# Understanding Mental Disorders

*Understanding Mental Disorders* aims to help current and future psychiatrists, and those who work with them, to think critically about the ethical, conceptual, and methodological questions that are raised by the theory and practice of psychiatry. It considers questions that concern the mind's relationship to the brain, the origins of our norms for thinking and behavior, and the place of psychiatry in medicine, and in society more generally. With a focus on the current debates around psychiatry's diagnostic categories, the authors ask where these categories come from, if psychiatry should be looking to find new categories that are based more immediately on observations of the brain, and whether psychiatrists need to employ any diagnostic categories at all. The book is a unique guide for readers who want to think carefully about the mind, mental disorders, and the practice of psychiatric medicine.

**Daniel Lafleur, MD, CM, FRCPC** is a clinical associate professor in the Department of Psychiatry at the University of British Columbia, Vancouver.

**Christopher Mole, BA (Hons), PhD** is a professor of philosophy, and chair of the Cognitive Systems Program, at the University of British Columbia, Vancouver.

**Holly Onclin, BA (Hons)** is a graduate of the Honours in Philosophy program at the University of British Columbia and a freelance illustrator in Vancouver.

# Understanding Mental Disorders

A Philosophical Approach to the Medicine of the Mind

Daniel Lafleur, Christopher Mole, and Holly Onclin

 Routledge
Taylor & Francis Group

NEW YORK AND LONDON

First published 2019
by Routledge
52 Vanderbilt Avenue, New York, NY 10017

and by Routledge
2 Park Square, Milton Park, Abingdon, Oxon, OX14 4RN

*Routledge is an imprint of the Taylor & Francis Group, an informa business*

*Library of Congress Cataloging-in-Publication Data*
Names: Lafleur, Daniel, author. | Mole, Christopher, 1979- author. | Onclin, Holly, author.
Title: Understanding mental disorders : a philosophical approach to the medicine of the mind / Daniel Lafleur, Christopher Mole, and Holly Onclin.
Description: New York, NY : Routledge, 2019. | Includes bibliographical references and index.
Identifiers: LCCN 2018056761 (print) | LCCN 2018057596 (ebook) | ISBN 9780429440496 (E-book) | ISBN 9781138340831 (hardback)
Subjects: | MESH: Mental Disorders | Psychiatry | Philosophy, Medical
Classification: LCC RC454 (ebook) | LCC RC454 (print) | NLM WM 100 | DDC 616.89--dc23
LC record available at https://lccn.loc.gov/2018056761

ISBN: 978-1-138-34083-1 (hbk)
ISBN: 978-1-138-34085-5 (pbk)
ISBN: 978-0-429-44049-6 (ebk)

Typeset in Adobe Garamond Pro

**Publisher's Note**
This book has been prepared from camera-ready copy provided by the authors.

À mes parents;

the members of the 2017 Psychiatry in Context Discussion Group;

and mom and dad.

# Contents

# List of Illustrations

# Preface

People living within a structure are often in a poor position to see how that structure was built. Those on the outside might have a clearer view, but if the structure enjoys some special status – on account of being esteemed, or empowered, or feared – then they might be reluctant to make any very close inspection of the foundations on which it rests. They might struggle to give a full account of the things that such an inspection reveals, and might struggle to get a fair hearing for any account that they do give, whether that account is troubling, or reassuring, or inconclusive.

Medicine – which is esteemed, empowered, and feared in varying measures – is one such structure.[1] Psychiatry, being the branch of medicine that is concerned with the mind, is a notably contentious part of it. From the inside the structure of psychiatric medicine is sometimes felt to shift disconcertingly, as the conceptual foundations on which it rests are worked on, but there never seems to be any real threat of it collapsing. Even if those on the outside do hear occasional creaks, and see the appearance of cracks, the people who are brought in to repair these always seem to be reassuringly professional. And the direst warnings about the structure's foundations were made so long ago that these no longer seem to be a matter of urgency.

The plan of those foundations – if there ever was a plan – nonetheless remains obscure. The foundations may yet prove to be sturdy ones. The difficulty is to find a vantage point from which they can be inspected, without prejudice or confusion, and without allowing ourselves to indulge in wishful thinking, or in truculent cynicism. This difficulty should be faced by those who work within the structure of psychiatric medicine, and by those whose business brings them near to it. It must also be faced by any theorist who would aspire to the building of some new structure, in a neighboring part of the same territory.

This book was written with all these groups of people in mind. It is a book for psychiatrists, and for other medical practitioners, who seek to plumb the conceptual depths of psychiatric diagnosis in a way that goes beyond what is called for in day-to-day practice. It is also a book for those who come into contact with the practice of psychiatric diagnosis in other ways, as patients and those who surround them, or as those who have an interest in studying psychiatric practice and its place in society. We do not attempt to give a full report, nor even a partial report, on the present condition of psychiatry's conceptual foundations, but we do try to bring those foundations more clearly into view, in a way that can help the reader to see the philosophical issues underpinning them.

Since medicine aspires to finding the causes for disease, inscribed somehow in the objective features of the body, the attempt to take a medical approach to the mind faces special difficulties. Unlike the other bodily phenomena that medicine must deal with, it seems that the mind must be understood, first of all, from the inside. This inside perspective on the mind needs to be brought into some sort of correspondence with the objective perspective of science. But the mind's relation to the body, and to the brain in particular, remains mysterious. There are good reasons why philosophers of mind have called the question of how subjective experiences relate to the brain "the hard problem."[2] That problem is no less hard when we meet a version of it in psychiatry, and it is further complicated by the fact that we encounter it in the company of various other problems, none of which is easy.

Those problems have various sources. Some are ethical, being concerned with the questions of what psychiatry should and should not do; some are metaphysical, being concerned with the fundamental question of what mental disorders *are*; others are epistemic, and are concerned with questions about the ways in which knowledge of a disordered mind can, and cannot, be acquired. The investigation of some of psychiatry's foundational issues requires the methods of scientific enquiry. Philosophical reflection cannot hope to resolve these issues by itself, but we hope to show that they are issues belonging to an area through which scientific enquiry and philosophical argumentation must proceed together. We focus, in particular, on psychiatric *diagnosis*, and on the medical and social status of the categories that are employed in it, these issues being at the heart of many current controversies.

The themes in this book emerged from a discussion group, which met during the early months of 2017. The group was for resident trainees in psychiatry at the University of British Columbia, and was facilitated by two of the authors (CM and DL). It provided an opportunity to discuss some of the philosophical issues that such students of psychiatry encounter, as they begin to make their professional home in this most peculiar of medical specialities. The authors would like to thank the UBC Department of Psychiatry, for providing logistical support for the group, and all the students who participated, for making it such a stimulating and enjoyable experience, without which this book would never have come to exist as it is now. Thanks are also due to Garson Leder, who completed a PhD in philosophy, under the supervision of one of us (CM), at the time when this book was being written. The influence of Garson's thinking about mental health is very gratefully acknowledged. The authors would also like to thank Steve Schlozman, who provided thoughtful advice on a draft of this book, and Aurelia Kong, whose help with typesetting software was invaluable. We also thank the Social Sciences and Humanities Research Council of Canada, which supported this project financially.

## Notes to Preface

1    This book takes the conceptual foundations of general medicine more or less for granted, and enquires into the position of psychiatry within it, as a branch of medicine that is somewhat unlike the other branches. The foundations of medicine more generally are critically examined by Jacob Stegenga in his 2018 book, *Medical Nihilism* (Oxford University Press).

2    It was David Chalmers who coined the phrase "The Hard Problem," in his 1995 paper, "Facing up to the problem of consciousness," published in *Journal of Consciousness Studies* 2, no 3 (1995):200–219.

# Part One: Mental Disorder

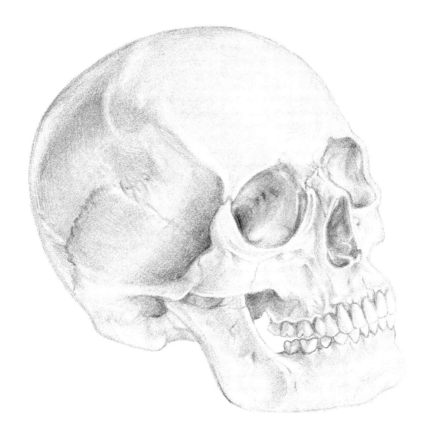

# Outline of Part One

### 1.1 What is Mental Disorder?

Mental disorders are diverse, in their origins and in their manifestations. One might even think that the category of "mental disorder" is too motley to be medically useful. That would be a mistake, since other branches of medicine address disorders that are no less diverse. Those branches of medicine are typically concerned with the various functions and malfunctions of some particular organ system. Psychiatry sometimes attempts to model itself on them, by taking itself to be that branch of medicine that is concerned with the mental functioning of the brain. Since this functioning is only partially understood, psychiatry finds itself in the vicinity of certain philosophical puzzles, among which the brain's ability to create conscious experiences is especially notable. The attempt to understand mental disorder therefore brings us up against some fundamental questions, which are unlike the questions raised by other branches of medicine.

### 1.2 What Makes a Mental Disorder *Mental?*

In our attempt to say what mental disorders are, we can start out with the broader category of disorders generally, and can then ask which of these disorders are the mental ones. This approach goes wrong if we take the mental disorders to be those that have mental consequences. It also goes wrong if we take the mental disorders to be those having mental causes. These criteria include too much or too little. A better answer can be given if we take the mental disorders to be those disorders to which a person's mind – construed broadly so as to include their thoughts, feelings, personality, and experiences – makes an ongoing explanatory contribution. But since all of the occasions on which the mind seems to be making such a contribution are cases in which an alternative explanation can be given, from which all talk of the mind has been removed, and replaced by talk of the biochemical processes taking place within the brain, the attempt to understand how a mind could possibly make any explanatory contribution leads us into another philosophical puzzle.

### 1.3 What Makes a Mental Disorder *Disordered?*

There are lots of ways in which one person's mind might be unlike the minds of others. Only some of these should be counted as mental disorders. But *which?* That question is morally important, since there are harms associated with diagnosing too many conditions, and harms associated with diagnosing too few. We would be giving the wrong answer to this question if the criteria by which we distinguished disorders from other conditions were specified only by reference to distress. We would also go wrong if we tried to operate with a purely biological criterion. Instead (following the official suggestion of the American Psychological Association's *Diagnostic and Statistical Manual*), this chapter proposes that mental disorders be understood as being those mental conditions that impede human flourishing, where "human flourishing" is understood to be something that is achievable in a social context. This proposal introduces a new set of complications, since it forces us to consider social factors on at least some of the occasions when we are deciding which conditions should be diagnosable.

# 1.1 What is Mental Disorder?

We sometimes learn, and sometimes we suspect, that a person suffers from a mental disorder. It might be some person with whom we live or work. It might be a friend, or a family member. It might even be oneself. There was a time, a generation ago, when people seldom talked about these disorders. Now that we do talk about them, it can be hard to know what is meant.

In order to know what we should make of mental disorders, and of the psychiatric practice in which they are diagnosed, we should like to have an account of what mental disorder *is*. The first part of this book therefore considers some of the approaches that might be taken to answering the question: "What is mental disorder?"[3]

A person who asks this question might be asking us to identify something that is *essential* to mental disorders. They might be wanting us to tell them about some one thing that all mental disorders have in common.[4]

They might then be disconcerted to discover how various the mental disorders are, with Alzheimer's dementia having nothing much in common with Gender dysphoria, and neither having much in common with Bipolar disorder, Post-traumatic stress disorder, or Narcissistic personality disorder. There are hundreds of mental disorders that a psychiatrist might diagnose.[5] The manifestations of these are quite diverse. So too are their origins.

Having noted this diversity, we might be tempted to think that this term – "mental disorder" – is unhelpful, being a term that bundles together things that are, in fact, quite different. If the term "mental disorder" can cover such very different things then it might seem that nothing specific has yet been said when a psychiatrist tells her patients that the disorders from which they suffer are mental ones. For the same reason it would seem that no precise field of enquiry has yet been defined when psychiatry sets itself the goal of understanding the mental disorders, and of finding treatments for them.

Although the diversity of their forms and origins might tempt us to give up on the idea of mental disorders, it would be too quick to reject that idea solely on these grounds. Diversity of forms and origins need not be a barrier to scientific enquiry. There are real differences between the wings of birds, and bats, and butterflies, and there are real differences between the ways in which these creatures' capacities for flight came into existence.[6] Such diversity should not lead us to abandon the very idea of wings, nor to give up on the project of saying what it is in virtue of which something qualifies as being a wing.

Even if the diversity of mental disorders is no less considerable, that diversity need not lead us to give up on the very idea of mental disorder, nor on the idea of studying these disorders scientifically. It should instead lead us to realize that – whether we are trying to say what a wing is or trying to say what a mental disorder is – we need to look at something other than the underlying substance of the things in question, and at something other than the ways in which these things come into existence.

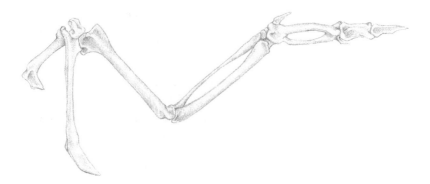

In saying this, we do not mean to suggest that the diversity of mental disorders creates no explanatory problems, only that these particular problems need not be special to psychiatry. Other branches of the life sciences cope with just as much diversity. So, too, do other branches of medicine. A liver specialist might need to treat some conditions that are genetic in origin, some that are caused by heavy drinking, and some that are the result of infections. This diversity in the processes leading to liver disorder is no reason to think that we would do well to give up on the very idea of "liver disorder." Nothing here should make hepatologists fear for the integrity of their discipline. A similar line of thinking suggests that psychiatrists need not be especially bothered by the diverse origins of *mental* disorder. That diversity might be a nuisance when we are asking what mental disorders are, but it would be a poor reason to give up on the very idea.

Although the theoretical challenges that originate in the diversity of mental disorders may be shared across the life sciences, there are other challenges that are more peculiarly psychiatric, and that are not shared by other branches of medicine. It has long been known that the brain plays a central role in the creation of the mind, but rather little is known about the way in which that role is to be explained. There are open questions about how it is that mental processes are grounded in the brain's physical properties, whether those mental processes are disorderly or not. Because these questions are open ones, our understanding of mental disorders is only loosely moored to any theory of their correspondences with the body. The field of psychiatry must therefore rely on some more abstract understanding of the mind. In place of the objective data that are given to other branches of medical science, psychiatry must work with subjective reports, from the people who suffer from mental disorders, and from the scientists and doctors who work with them. Whatever our enthusiasm for the help that psychiatric treatments might provide, and whatever our qualms about the use of such treatments, we should admit that minds are peculiar topics of scientific enquiry, and peculiar targets for medical intervention, in a way that livers, hearts, and lungs are not.

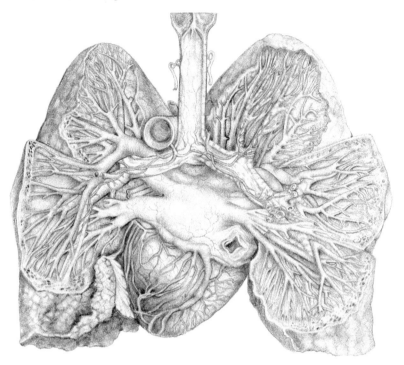

It is because of this peculiarity that our attempts to understand psychiatry lead us from the domain of medicine, which is illuminated by the evidence of anatomy and physiology, into the more forbidding territory of philosophy. We shall be exploring this path between psychiatry and philosophy throughout the chapters that follow.

We can make a start on this exploration – but only a start – by seeing how far we can go while thinking of psychiatry as being on a par with the other branches of medicine.[7]

Many branches of medicine focus on the disorders of some one organ system.[8] A hepatologist is concerned with the liver, an ophthalmologist with the eyes, a nephrologist with the kidneys. When kidneys go wrong, in their various ways and for their various reasons, the result is one or other sort of renal disorder, which a nephrologist may or may not be able to treat. When eyes go wrong, in equally diverse ways and for equally diverse reasons, the result is one or other sort of visual disorder, which an ophthalmologist may or may not be able to cure, or, if not cure, then at least correct.

We might hope to make a start in our understanding of psychiatry by noting that, although minds are special for any number of reasons, the brains that support them are biological organs, and these cannot be immune from malfunction. Brains, like other organs, must go wrong sometimes, even if their going wrong need not take the form of some readily observable wound or contusion. When they do go wrong – in their various ways and for their various reasons – the result will, often enough, be one or other mental disorder, which a psychiatrist may or may not be able to cure, to treat, or to correct.

This analogy between psychiatry and the other branches of medicine seems on the face of it like a good one. Pursuing it leads to the suggestion that we might consider mental disorders as "disorders of brain function," just as renal disorders are disorders of kidney function, and cardiac disorders are disorders of the heart. This would not be completely wrong. Nor would it be entirely satisfactory.[9]

One reason to be dissatisfied with this suggestion is that it would give the impression that psychiatry is straightforwardly a branch of brain science. It would therefore ignore the distinction between *psychiatry*, which is the medicine of the mind, and *neurology*, which is the branch of medicine in which disorders of the brain (and of the nervous system more generally) are studied. Psychiatrists do have special reasons to be interested in the brain, but – unlike neurologists – they are generally concerned with the brain only insofar as it is the basis for our thoughts, moods, experiences, feelings, and actions. We know that the brain *is* the basis for these various thoughts, moods, and feelings, but we do not know how, and the puzzles concerning that relationship are unlike puzzles concerning the functioning of other organs.[10] No organ's function has ever been easy to discern.[11] It took centuries of enquiry before we could understand the functioning of the heart, lungs, and liver,[12] but now that we do know what their functions are, we can see how it is that these various organs accomplish those functions. The relationship of brains to minds is exceptional, in part because it is *philosophically* puzzling.

Having looked at a heart, and having investigated its parts, we can understand how hearts might be suitable for the pumping of blood. Having examined lungs, we can understand how a pair of these might be suitable for absorbing something from the air.[13]

When our attempts to understand the mind take us into the skull, this sense of understanding gives out. On examining the white and gray matter of a brain, we encounter something that is more puzzling than the pump of the heart, or the bellows of the lungs. Our exploration does not enable us to see how these loose lobes of flesh might sustain our hopes, fears, feelings, or beliefs. To understand that, a different sort of enquiry would seem to be needed.

For all the philosophical puzzlement that is associated with it, this enquiry into the brain's relationship to the mind can claim to have made some recent progress. The mystery of a brain's capacity to support the mind was somewhat mitigated when it was discovered that the fatty flesh from which brains are made is a special sort of flesh, composed of quite peculiar cells, many of which are capable of transmitting electrochemical signals.[14] That discovery was made in the 1950s, at just the time when a sudden acceleration was taking place in our ability to use such signals for the processing of information, and so for the performance of computations. A huge amount of research has since been devoted to the question of how a mind's features might be explained by taking these features to be the result of computations that are taking place within and between the cells from which a brain is made.

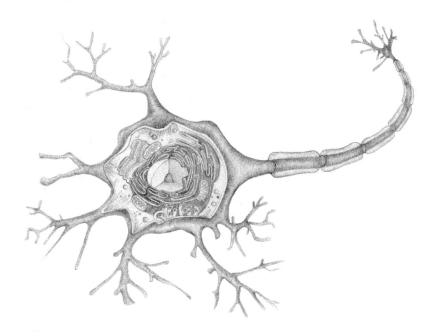

Although it has limitations, the idea that nerve cells perform computations is the most fruitful idea about brain function that we currently have. It removes some of the mysteries concerning the ability of brain cells to sustain a mind.

It also provides some explanation for the fact that psychiatry is such a singular branch of medicine. The processing of information is unlike the processing of bile or of blood. It can go wrong without any physical perturbation, and without this malfunction leaving any chemical trace.[15] The physics and chemistry of a computer will be just the same, whether or not the software running on that computer is faulty. The physics and chemistry of a brain might be similarly unchanged, whether or not there are disorders in the mind that this brain is supporting. To the extent that psychiatric disorders are disorders of the brain's information processing, psychiatric medicine need not proceed via a treatment of wounds, nor even via a redressing of chemical imbalances. That is one way in which psychiatry and the other branches of medicine might differ.

Although the idea that brain cells perform computations has proven to be fruitful, it cannot by itself solve all of the mysteries concerning the mind's relationship to the brain. The idea that some set of computations can sustain our hopes and fears is, by itself, only somewhat less mysterious than the idea that those hopes and fears are sustained by a lump of convoluted flesh.[16] We can see this by remembering that there are a great many things with the capacity to transmit information-carrying signals, and with the capacity to perform computations on them. This capacity is shared by silicon chips, vacuum tubes, telephone exchanges, and transistor radios. Since there is no reason to suppose that telephone exchanges or vacuum tubes are the subjects of their own hopes, desires, moods, or personalities, there is work remaining to be done before a brain's capacity for the transmission and storage of information can be said to *explain* the mind's capacity for the having of thoughts.[17]

One quite particular explanatory difficulty originates in the fact that, unlike the information-bearing states of computers, our thoughts are at least sometimes *conscious*. Philosophers have had a lot to say about this.[18] The explanatory difficulty that results from it arises, in one form or another, whether we are trying to give an explanation for moods, for desires, for hopes, or for any of the other familiar denizens of the mind.[19] This is a difficulty that has been brought to light most clearly in connection with the explanation of perceptual experiences, such as you are having now, in perceiving the look, feel, and smell of this book.

If you have friends who are profoundly blind, and who have been blind for all of their lives, then you will probably have wondered whether there is anything you can do that will convey to them what the experience of seeing is like. A profoundly blind person will of course realize that sighted people have some additional way of knowing about their surroundings, other than by hearing, smelling, feeling, or tasting. They will understand that this additional way of knowing enables those of us with vision to simultaneously encounter a large array of things, having various shapes, sizes, and locations. They will realize that this way of knowing does not present us with the pitch, tone, or timbre of things, in the way that hearing must, nor with their flavors, temperatures, aromas, or weights.

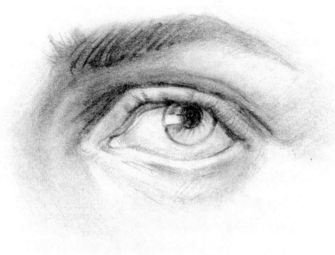

Although a blind person can know all these things about vision, it seems that they will still need to make some sort of imaginative leap before they have a grasp on what the experience of seeing is like. Perhaps it would help for them to learn more about the retina, and about the information processing that takes place in the visual cortex. There are plenty of blind people who know about all of that. But even after this knowledge is acquired, it is still tempting to think that something might be missing from their appreciation of what the experience of vision is like.[20] A blind person may be sufficiently imaginative to make the necessary leap of thought. The point to notice is that there is a leap needing to be made. It is hard for us, and no less hard for the blind person, to know whether it has been made successfully.

It is not easy to put one's finger on what it is that might be missing from the congenitally blind person's appreciation of what vision is like, after this person has learned about the brain's full range of visual mechanisms, but before any imaginative leap has been accomplished. If we *could* put our finger on what this missing thing is, we would then be on the way to finding words to express it, and so we could begin to tell the blind person what it is that they have been lacking. We can nonetheless bring this missing thing somewhat more clearly into focus by thinking, in particular, about the blind person's understanding of *color*.

The explanation of colors seems to be a particular sticking point in our attempt to convey to a blind person what visual experiences are like. Having noticed this, it becomes clear that a version of our problem occurs, not only for the profoundly and congenitally blind, but also for those who are merely

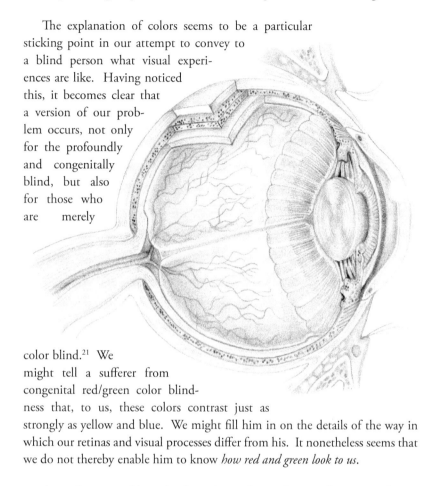

color blind.[21] We might tell a sufferer from congenital red/green color blindness that, to us, these colors contrast just as strongly as yellow and blue. We might fill him in on the details of the way in which our retinas and visual processes differ from his. It nonetheless seems that we do not thereby enable him to know *how red and green look to us*.

An analogous problem also faces those of us with normal vision. Whereas human color vision is normally mediated by three kinds of wavelength-specific light receptors on our retinas, it has been discovered that there are four kinds in the eyes of goldfish.[22] And it is likely that five kinds are active in the eyes of a pigeon.[23] Since there are corresponding differences in the processes that take place in the visual parts of their brains, it seems that these animals see more colors than we do, much as most of us see more colors than those who are color blind.

By studying their retinas and visual cortices, we can come to understand *what* it is that these creatures are able to see: the pigeon is able to see patterns that we are not able to see in, for example, flower-petals; and the goldfish is able to see contrasts that we are not able to see in the ultraviolet frequencies of light. Understanding a goldfish's eyes, and the computations taking place in its brain, enables us to know *what* it is that the fish visually encounters, via its additional dimensions of color. But understanding all of this still seems to leave us without any understanding of *what these colors look like for the goldfish*.

In each of these cases it is an understanding of what experiences are *like* that seems to be elusive. It is a fact about what visual experiences are like that we struggle to get across to the profoundly blind person. It is a fact about what our color experiences are like that we struggle to get across to those who are color blind. And it is a fact of the same sort that we are left wondering about, when we encounter creatures with sensory capacities that are richer than our own.

Philosophers have dubbed these hard-to-understand properties of experience "qualia," that being the Latin plural of "what it is like."[24] They have argued, as philosophers will, over whether the term is a good one.

These qualia seem to be at the root of the problems that we encounter, when we are trying to give an account of the mind's relationship to the brain. Understanding the information processing that is taking place in a person's brain goes some way toward explaining their experiences. But, as an explanation for the fact that this brain supports experiences that are *like something* for the person in question, an account of the brain's information processing seems to stop short.

This gap in our understanding places an upper bound on the explanatory accomplishments for any theory of mental disorder: we might expect the theory of some mental disorder to provide us with an account of the way in which the features and symptoms of that disorder arise and interact, but we should not expect the theory to reveal the consciously experienced character of what it is like to have that disorder.[25] To get into a position where we can appreciate such consciously experienced character, something more like an exercise in imaginative understanding – and less like an exercise in scientific explanation – will be required.

# Notes to Chapter 1.1

3     The question 'What is mental disorder?' admits of various answers, and – like all questions of the form 'What is *x*?' – it is subject to various interpretations. It is, nonetheless, a natural question to ask, not only for psychiatrists and their patients, but also for parents, researchers, and for people who are going through extraordinary stressful experiences. The question has a primary place in George Graham's *The Disordered Mind: An Introduction to Philosophy of Mind and Mental Illness* (Routledge), a book that provides a useful introduction to many of the topics that we discuss here. Graham takes the heterogeneity of mental disorders to indicate that this question is a daunting one (p. 19).

The American Psychiatric Association's official answers to the question of what mental disorder is are reviewed in a 2010 article by D.J. Stein, K.A. Phillips, D. Bolton, K.W.M. Fulford, J.Z. Sadler & K.S. Kendler: "What is a mental/psychiatric disorder? From DSM-IV to DSM-V." *Psychological Medicine* 40, no 11 (2010): 1759–1765.

There is evidence that, in the minds of at least some sectors of the general public, the status of the concept of mental disorder is contentious. Evidence for this can be seen in Nicolas Rüsch, Sara Evans-Lacko, and Graham Thornicroft's 2012 article "What is a mental illness? Public views and their effects on attitudes and disclosure." *Australian & New Zealand Journal of Psychiatry* 46, no. 7 (2012): 641–650. Rüsch and his colleagues conducted a large-scale survey of people in the UK, and found there to be varying levels of agreement with the idea that Depression, Bipolar disorder, and Schizophrenia are mental illnesses.

4     There are a number of different suppositions that might motivate the idea that psychiatry should be able to identify some one essence, which all the mental disorders share (and in virtue of which they all belong together, in this one category of "mental disorders"). Those who endorse such an idea might be supposing that "mental disorder" is a natural kind term, in the sense of "natural kind" that is identified in the *Stanford Encyclopedia of Philosophy*: "To say that a kind is *natural* is to say that it corresponds to a grouping that reflects the structure of the natural world rather than the interests and actions of human beings." We have more to say about natural kinds, and about non-natural ones, in Part Three of this book.

5     The hundreds of psychiatric diagnoses have been enumerated in two separate catalogs: the American Psychiatric Association's *Diagnostic and Statistical Manual* (about which we have more to say later in this book), and Chapter V of the World Health Organization's *International Classification of Diseases*.

6    The idea that different species might independently evolve the same traits, with each finding a different way to implement that trait, was already clear to Charles Darwin and Alfred Russel Wallace, at the time when the theory of evolution by natural selection was being proposed. It can be seen in the discussion of "Analogical or adaptive characters," which can be found in Chapter XIII of Darwin's 1859 masterwork, *The Origin of Species*.

The significance of such convergent evolution is discussed by George McGee in his 2011 book, *Convergent Evolution: Limited Forms Most Beautiful* (MIT Press). Details of several routes to the evolution of flight can be found in Ulla Norberg's majestic 1990 book *Vertebrate Flight: Mechanics, Physiology, Morphology, Ecology and Evolution* (Springer-Verlag).

7    The suggestion that psychiatry be thought of as being on a par with other branches of medicine is often referred to as "the medical model" (a title under which that suggestion is often debated, and often attacked). This suggestion is defended by Samuel B. Guze, in his 1992 book, *Why Psychiatry is a Branch of Medicine* (Oxford University Press).

A representative sample of the different occasions on which the medical model of psychiatry has been reappraised can be found in:

Gerald L. Klerman. "Mental illness, the medical model, and psychiatry." *The Journal of Medicine and Philosophy* 2, no. 3 (1977): 220–243;

Gordon Claridge. *Origins of Mental Illness: Temperament, Deviance and Disorder* (Basil Blackwell, 1985);

James E. Madduz. "Stopping the 'madness': Positive psychology and the deconstruction of the illness ideology and the DSM." In C.R. Snyder and Shane J. Lopez (eds.) *Handbook of Positive Psychology*, 13–25 (Oxford University Press, 2001);

Meredith F. Small. *The Culture of Our Discontent: Beyond the Medical Model of Mental Illness* (National Academies Press, 2006);

Shane N. Glackin. "Tolerance and illness: The politics of medical and psychiatric classification." *Journal of Medicine and Philosophy* 35, no. 4 (2010): 449–465;

Philip Thomas, Patrick Bracken, and Sami Timimi. "The limits of evidence-based medicine in psychiatry." *Philosophy, Psychiatry & Psychology* 19, no. 4 (2012): 295–308.

8    People who have mental disorders are often resistant to the idea that they are ipso facto *sick*. They are therefore resistant to the idea that mental

disorders should be thought of as diseases. There may indeed be good reasons to resist these ideas. It would, however, be a mistake to think that resistance to them brings with it any commitment to the rejection of the idea that psychiatry is properly thought of as a branch of medicine.

That is because branches of medicine need not concern themselves exclusively with diseases, or with sickness: Medicine can quite properly be concerned with all sorts of allergies, ailments, conditions, complaints, and infirmities. The question of whether psychiatric disorders are appropriate occasions for medical intervention can therefore be separated from the question of whether those disorders are properly thought of as diseases, and it can be separated, in the same way, from the question of whether the suffering caused by these disorders should be considered a form of sickness. We can therefore separate the question of whether addiction (for example) is a disease, from the question of whether addiction is best treated as a medical problem.

9      The distinction between mental disorders and brain disorders is a distinction that allows for many borderline cases. The two categories are not mutually exclusive. The distinction between them is nonetheless a contentious one, since it is often taken to mark the boundary of a physician's professional jurisdiction, with the brain disorders cast as properly neurological problems, and the disorders of the mind as psychiatric ones.

It is sometimes suggested that the very idea of drawing a distinction between these two categories is obviously wrong headed, since the mind and the brain are not distinct. That suggestion is an oversimplification, since even things that are not distinct might go wrong in different ways. The sculpture that has been crafted from a lump of stone might be defective as a sculpture – perhaps because the hands are too big – without there being anything defective about the stone, considered as a stone. In general, the fact that X is made entirely from Y does not entail that defects in X are defects of Y.

A recent discussion of the way in which a distinction can be drawn between mental disorders and brain disorders can be found in Anneli Jefferson's 2018 article "What does it take to be a brain disorder?" *Synthese* (online first, April 2018).

10    The current phase of philosophical disputes about the mind's relation to the brain was initiated in the middle of the 1950s, in the works of Ullin T. Place, Herbert Feigl, and Jack Smart. Their seminal papers are:

Ullin T. Place. "Is consciousness a brain process?" *British Journal of Psychology* 47, no. 1 (1956): 44–50;

Herbert Feigl. "The 'mental' and the 'physical'." *Minnesota Studies in the Philosophy of Science* 2 (1958): 370–497;

Jack J.C. Smart. "Sensations and brain processes." *Philosophical Review* 68, no. 2 (April 1959): 141–156.

These works set the agenda for a lot of the philosophical research that has been done in the last half century, both in the philosophy of mind, and in the philosophy of language.

It is probably an oversimplification to suppose that the mind and the brain are one and the same thing. That would imply that you cannot possibly have one without the other, which seems to be wrong: Your brain will still *exist*, although it will not any longer be active, even after your mind has ceased to exist. (Perhaps we should say, instead, that the mind is the result of some of the things that the brain *does*.) The problems that are faced by any attempt to simply *identify* mental states with brain states received a brilliant and influential exposition in Saul Kripke's *Naming and Necessity* (Harvard University Press, 1980).

11    Although it might seem obvious to us that the heart pumps the blood, while the liver cleans and maintains it, these things did not seem obvious until a great deal of scientific work had been done. It is often said that Aristotle took the heart to be the seat of the mind, and took the brain's function to be the cooling of the blood. His colleague Theophrastus takes him to have thought as much, and he certainly does seem to take such a position in his treatise on *Sense and Sensibilia*. He does so on the grounds that the heart appeared to be better connected with the various sense organs and muscles. (The nervous system had not yet been identified.) Aristotle suggests a somewhat more complicated position in Book II of his treatise on *The Parts of Animals*. According to the picture that we find there the heart and the brain work together to produce mental phenomena, with the heart's contributions tending to be heat-increasing, and the brain's tending to counterbalance these. This treatise as a whole exemplifies Aristotle's sophistication as a scientific observer. It should be read, together with *Sense and Sensibilia,* by anyone who is tempted to suppose that the scientific method is a product of modernity.

For an account of the difficulties that had to be surmounted, before the functions of the various organs could be established, see Charles Singer's book,

*A Short History of Anatomy and Physiology from the Greeks to Harvey* (Dover Books, 1957).

12    The lungs that are depicted on p. 7 are based on an illustration in Jean-Marc Bourgery and Nicolas Henri Jacob's *Anatomie de l'homme* (Guerin, 1862). Thanks to Michel Royon, the original image can be found on Wikimedia commons.

13    The kidney depicted on p. 8 is based on an 1885 dictionary etching by Paul Labarthe. The heart on p. 9 is based on an illustration from Carl Ernst Bock's 1879 *Atlas of Human Anatomy* (Kraufsu & Eltzner).

14    Luigi Galvani (1737–1798) was the first to realize that electric impulses were involved in enabling nerve cells to pass signals to one another. Speculations about the way in which such impulses might carry information date from the end of the nineteenth century, with the physiologist Henry Pickering Bowditch suggesting that nerve impulses might be analogous to the dots and dashes in the Morse code that was then used for the transmission of telegraph signals. The properties of neurons that enable them to transmit signals were first studied in detail in the 1950s, by Warren McCulloch and Walter Pitts, at about the time when Claude Shannon was formalizing his mathematical theory of information transmission (Shannon, 1948), and when Alan Turing was showing how the concept of computation could be mathematically formalized (Turing, 1936), and could then be applied to the philosophy of mind (Turing, 1950). The clearest synthesis of these ideas was given by John von Neumann, in his posthumously published 1958 book, *The Computer and the Brain* (Yale University Press).

15    The point that computational problems need not correspond to any physical or chemical abnormality is made by David Papineau in his 1994 paper "Mental disorder, illness and biological disfunction." *Royal Institute of Philosophy Supplements* 37 (1994): 73–82. The same point can be found in George Graham's *The Disordered Mind: An Introduction to Philosophy of Mind and Mental Illness,* on page 23.

16    The idea that a brain's computational properties explain its ability to create a mind is a foundational assumption for most of cognitive science. As a philosophical theory, it was elaborated by Hilary Putnam in his 1967 article on "The mental life of some machines," published in Hector-Neri Castañeda (ed.), *Intentionality, Minds and Perception* (Wayne State University Press). The philosophical literature on this idea has grown to be vast. A now-classic philosophical attack on the adequacy of this idea was given by John Searle, in his 1990 article "Is the brain's mind a computer program?" *Scientific American* 262,

no. 1 (1990): 25–31. Tim Maudlin raises a no-less important objection to computational explanations in his "Computation and consciousness." *The Journal of Philosophy* 86, no. 8: 407–432.

17    This influential line of thought was first explored by Ned Block, in his 1978 paper "Troubles with functionalism." *Minnesota Studies in the Philosophy of Science* 9 (1978): 261–325.

18    The difficulty of explaining the consciousness of our thoughts was made vivid by Thomas Nagel, in his 1974 paper "What is it like to be a bat?" *Philosophical Review* 83, no. 4 (1974): 435–450. That difficulty is faced directly in Daniel C. Dennett's 1991 book *Consciousness Explained* (Little, Brown & Co.). Rather different arguments concerning the possibility of addressing this difficulty can be found in David J. Chalmers' 1996 book *The Conscious Mind* (Oxford University Press).

The philosophical tradition to which these works contribute is, of course, an ancient one. Writing in the third century BCE, Aristotle's successor Theophrastus considers the pre-Socratic phase of that tradition. When he writes, "It is strange, furthermore, to insist that to all those who perceive the same things there comes the same subjective appearance" (section. 70), he is pursuing a line of thought very much like that which we are following here. For discussion, see George Stratton's 1917 book *Theophrastus and the Greek Physiological Psychology before Aristotle* (G. Allen and Unwin).

19    There is some controversy about whether a person's beliefs manifest themselves in that person's stream of consciousness, in the way that their perceptual experiences typically do. Our remarks here are not intended to take sides in that controversy, detailed discussion of which can be found in a 2011 book, edited by Tim Bayne and Michelle Montague: *Cognitive Phenomenology* (Oxford University Press).

20    The line of thought being elaborated here is a version of that which Frank Jackson elaborated in his much-discussed "Knowledge Argument." Jackson's original presentations of that argument can be found in his 1982 article, "Epiphenomenal qualia." *Philosophical Quarterly* 32, no. 127 (1982): 127–136, and again, from a slightly different perspective, in his 1986 sequel to that paper, "What Mary didn't know." *The Journal of Philosophy* 83, no. 5 (1985): 291–295.

A representative sample of recent thinking about Jackson's argument, and about some of the issues related to it, can be found in a 2006 volume edited by Torin Alter and Sven Walter: *Phenomenal Concepts and Phenomenal Knowledge: New Essays on Consciousness and Physicalism* (Oxford University Press).

A line of thinking that is very similar to the one that we are pursuing here makes an earlier appearance in John Locke's (1690) *An Essay Concerning Human Understanding* (a book about which we have more to say in Part Three). In his discussion of the way in which language can be used to express simple ideas, Locke writes:

> A studious blind man who had mightily beaten his head about visible objects, and made use of the explication of his books and friends to understand those names of light and colours which often came in his way, bragged one day that he now understood what "scarlet" signified. Upon which his friend demanding, what scarlet was? the blind man answered, It was like the sound of a trumpet! Just such an understanding of the name of any other simple idea will he have who hopes to get it only from a definition, or other words made use of to explain it. (p. 345)

21    The version of this point that arises in connection with color blindness is discussed in Knut Nordby's 2007 piece "What is this thing you call color: Can a totally color-blind person know about color?" published in Torin Alter and Sven Walter (eds.) *Phenomenal Concepts and Phenomenal Knowledge: New Essays on Consciousness and Physicalism* (Oxford University Press).

22    The ability of fish to see more colors than humans can is documented by Ron Douglas and Mustafa Djamgoz in their 1990 book, *The Visual System of Fish* (Chapman and Hall).

23    Jacky Emmerton and Juan D. Delhis provide evidence for the super-human visual capacities of pigeons in their article "Wavelength discrimination in the 'visible' and ultraviolet spectrum by pigeons." *Journal of Comparative Physiology* 141, no. 1 (1980): 47–52.

24    The term "qualia" seems to have been coined by C.I. Lewis, in his 1929 book *Mind and the World Order* (Charles Scribner and Sons). The idea is criticized by Georges Rey in his article "A narrow representationalist account of qualitative experience." *Philosophical Perspectives* 12 (1998): 435–458, and also by Daniel C. Dennett, in several places. These include Dennett's 1994 paper, "Instead of qualia," originally published in Antti Revonsuo and Matti Kamppinen (eds.) *Consciousness in Philosophy and Cognitive Neuroscience* (Lawrence Erlbaum), 129–139. That paper is reproduced as Chapter Eight of Dennett's 1998 book, *Brainchildren: Essays on Designing Minds* (MIT Press).

25    Although the point that we are making here may have a special importance for psychiatric medicine, a version of it can also be applied to any other branch of medicine. The need for imagination, in coming to an understanding

of what psychiatric disorders are like for their sufferers, is paralleled by the need for imagination, in coming to an understanding of what other disorders are like for *their* sufferers. The qualia of the experience of tonsillitis are no more empirically tractable than are the qualia of the experience of Schizophrenia. If the felt-experience of tonsillitis is easier to understand, that is not because it is easier to capture in a scientific theory.

# 1.2 What Makes a Mental Disorder *Mental*?

By starting from the idea that brains sustain minds, and do so by performing computations, we have seen that there is some reason to give up on the idea that mental disorders must always correspond to imbalances in the chemistry or physics of the brain, which a psychiatrist could treat, just as the cardiologist treats disturbances in the heart.

This does not imply that mental disorders are never a matter of chemical imbalance. There is no need to suppose that mental disorders must *always* be, or always not be, the result of chemical imbalances, or of physical perturbations. Disruption in one sort of process may or may not lead to a disruption in the other. The finding that there is such a disruption may or may not suggest a possible course of treatment, or a route by which that disruption could be corrected. We would need to consider evidence in any particular case.

Having noted this – and having also noted that there is no need to identify any single origin or essence that is shared by all of the mental disorders – our original question remains in need of an answer: What *is* mental disorder? What does it mean if a doctor says that you have one?

We can approach these questions via a two-step route,[26] by first asking what it is that makes a disorder *mental*, and then asking what it is that makes some condition of the mind *disordered*.

One might hope to answer the first of these questions by saying that the mental disorders are those disorders that have mental symptoms among their effects.[27] This much seems like it must surely be correct. But, since we are trying to say what mental disorder *is,* to have said this much is not yet to have said enough.

That is because a disorder might cause mental symptoms but *not* be a mental disorder. Consider the disorder of an overactive thyroid gland. This is primarily a disorder of the body. It is caused by a gland in the neck, when that gland produces an excess of hormone. Although hyperthyroidism is a bodily disorder, and not a mental one, it does typically manifest itself mentally, in a nervous and edgy mood.

Other disorders of the body can also manifest themselves in the contours of their sufferer's mental life. Any condition that results in a loss of sleep might cause pessimism. Any condition that results in ongoing pain might cause irritability. If we included all of these conditions within the category of "mental disorders" then this category would become an almost useless one: it would apply to almost any medical condition, and so the application of it to some particular condition would tell us nothing distinctive about it. If the idea of "mental disorder" is going to be used to tell us something that is useful and distinctive, then it cannot be that the having of mental symptoms is what qualifies a disorder as being mental. Our account of what it is that makes the mental disorders mental will therefore have to come from somewhere else.

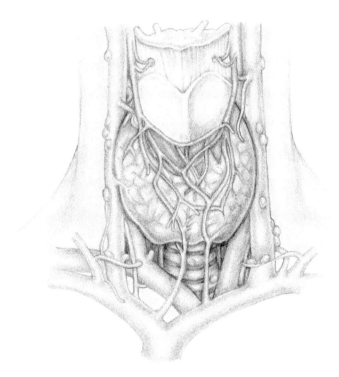

Having seen that we would be including too many conditions in the category of mental disorders if we were to say that disorders qualify as mental on account of having mental *effects*, we might instead try saying that disorders qualify as mental on account of having mental *causes*. This might be a step in the right direction, but saying only this would give us the opposite problem. It would include too few conditions.

Schizophrenia and Major depressive episodes should certainly be included in the category of mental disorders. But cases of Schizophrenia might be brought about by a combination of genetic, epigenetic, and environmental factors. And episodes of depression might sometimes be triggered by a lack of exposure to sunlight, by a hormone imbalance after giving birth, or by the consequences of a head injury. All sorts of mental and physical things can cause a mind to become disordered.

Since mental disorders need not have mental causes, and since non-mental disorders can sometimes have mental effects, neither causes nor effects can give us the answer, by themselves, to our question of what it is that makes mental disorders mental. We should not give up on the idea that mental disorders do indeed have mental causes and effects. That idea must at least be partially right, even if we have seen that it does not give the answer to our question by itself. If we are to develop this idea in a more promising direction, we need to adopt a more nuanced picture of the ways in which causes and effects can operate.

Rather than thinking of mental disorders as being those that have down-stream mental consequences – which would, we have seen, include too much – and rather than thinking of mental disorders as being those that have upstream mental causes – which would, we have seen, include too little – we might do better to think of mental disorders as being those disorders that develop in a way that is explicable only if the *ongoing contribution* of mental events is considered, where the mental events making these ongoing contributions might be specific contentful thoughts, or might be more general occurrences, involving various deficits of normal mental function. Rather than being the initiating trigger of mental disorders, these various mental events should be thought of as making an ongoing contribution to the way in which the mental disorders come about, to the way in which they manifest themselves, and to the way in which they pass off, or become entrenched.[28] To say this is to imply that mental disorders need not *originate* in the mind. The mind must, however, be mentioned in any complete account of the way in which these disorders manifest, develop, or persist.[29]

At the center of this proposal is the idea that *ongoing causal processes*, rather than isolatable triggers or outcomes, should be thought of as crucial. Taking this idea seriously requires that our picture of the causes and effects of a mental disorder be one in which there is a web of ongoing causal interactions. The causes and effects that participate in these interactions will not be organized into a straightforward chain, with one thing transmitting energy to another, which in turn brings about a third.[30] Instead they will involve sustained processes of facilitation, inhibition, catalysis, and prevention. These processes differ from the chain-like causal processes that we see playing out on a billiard table, where the event of one ball's being struck causes the subsequent event of some other ball's motion to the pocket. Although billiard balls provide a simple model, which can sometimes help us to think clearly about causal relationships, that model is not going to be helpful here.

By recognizing the causal complexities of mental disorder, we are able to give a better account of the things that a causally simplified approach got wrong. We are able to say that – although a long bout of flu may cause one to feel hopeless and pessimistic – this does not imply that the flu should be counted as a mental disorder. Cases of flu will fail to qualify as mental disorders, even if they have a significant effect on one's mood, provided that mental causes need not be mentioned when we are giving an explanation for the development of the influenza infection, and of the body's response to it. We can say this while still recognizing that hopelessness or pessimism can sometimes qualify as being the symptoms of a mental disorder, even in cases where a bout of flu exacerbates them.

Shifting to this more complex picture of causation also enables us to classify hyperthyroidism as a bodily disorder, rather than a mental one, as we have seen that we should. The reasoning here is much the same as in the case of flu: The mental consequences of hyperthyroidism do not themselves contribute to the disordered amount of hormone that is being produced by the patient's thyroid gland. That is entirely the result of some physically explicable failure in the patient's hormone regulation. This dysfunction has mental consequences, but those consequences make no ongoing contribution to the way in which the thyroid condition develops, nor to the way in which it becomes entrenched. An excess of thyroid hormone therefore qualifies as a *bodily* disorder, even though it is a disorder with mental symptoms.

By thinking of mental disorders as being disorders to the development of which mental factors make an ongoing contribution – and by avoiding the idea that mental disorders are all and only those disorders that have mental triggers or mental outcomes – we are also able to get away from the idea that the category of mental disorders and the category of bodily disorders are clearly separable. There is a possibility of overlap between these categories. The area of their overlap might turn out to be large.

Because the categories of mental and bodily disorder can overlap, being told that one's disorder is mental does not imply that that disorder is not also bodily. The bodily and mental aspects of a disorder might interact closely. There is no general reason to think that the bodily symptoms of mental disorders are of secondary importance, nor to think that two different senses of "suffer" are in play when we say that patients suffer from bodily symptoms, and also suffer from mental ones. It is sometimes said that mental disorders are "all in the mind," but if the suggestion that we have been developing here is correct then this "all" is, on at least some occasions, misplaced. The mind might only be one part of the story.

Although the suggestion that we have been exploring gives us the right verdicts in a range of different cases, it also brings us up against a philosophical puzzle. That puzzle is concerned with the question of whether, and how, any *mental* mechanism could ever exert an ongoing influence on the physical realm.

On those occasions when mental mechanisms would appear to be making a contribution to the development of some patient's condition, the claim that it really is a *mental* mechanism that makes this contribution can always seem to be threatened by the prospect of an alternative explanation being given – without mentioning mental entities at all – by instead describing the processes that are occurring at the neural, or at the biochemical, level.

We know enough about the mind's relationship to the brain to know that, whenever there is some change in a person's mood, *something* corresponding to this change must be going on in that person's brain. (If nothing were changing in their brain then it would be quite mysterious how this change in mood could make any difference at all to the things that the person says and does.) We also know that, whatever this change in the brain happens to be on any particular occasion, it will always be something that could be described in the vocabulary of chemistry and biology. This biochemical description enables us to see how the events taking place in the brain are governed by the laws of nature. But having seen that these brain events were events the occurrence of which was governed by biochemical laws, there no longer seems to be any genuine contribution for the *mental* life of the person to make. It now seems that we could give a complete explanation for some change in mood using *only* the biochemical vocabulary. The biochemical processes corresponding to the person's change of mood therefore seem to be the real causes of it. Any mental contribution comes to seem irrelevant. [31]

We could say the same thing about *any* change of mood. We could also say it about any other change to which a mental state seems to contribute. We therefore face the question of how mental occurrences can ever cause anything: How can these mental occurrences be anything other than a side effect of something that is merely biochemical, and that therefore operates according to laws that are, ultimately, merely physical? If they cannot then it would seem to be impossible for there to be any genuine mental disorders, in the sense of "mental disorder" that we have been exploring.

The puzzle that these questions raise is a puzzle about mental causation quite generally, and not a puzzle about mental disorder in particular. It arises from the difficulty of saying how mental events can exert any genuine influence in the physical world. It is a relatively straightforward matter to describe how one billiard ball can interact with another by colliding with it, and it is only a little less straightforward to describe the way in which one ongoing physical process can play a role in the continuous modulation of another. The thing that remains a mystery is how billiard balls, cues, and the hands that hold them, could possibly be set in motion by, or have their motion modulated by, our thoughts about them.

It is worth taking a moment to notice that the problem raised by these questions has nothing to do with free will.[32] It is a problem that occurs whenever something happens in a person's life that seems to be influenced by the operation of that person's mind. This problem arises whenever a mood, belief, urge, or obsession, seems to be the cause of some change. It does not depend on the things that are influenced by these beliefs and urges being things that are freely chosen. Even in those cases where we do *not* experience ourselves as free – where an obsession has us in its grip, or a mood comes over us suddenly – the same problem arises. The problem is about mental causation quite generally, and not only about a sort of causation that is involved in cases of free will. It arises because it is hard to see how mental events can *ever* cause things, whether or not an exercise of free will occurs when they do so.

We should also note that this particular problem does not depend on any suppositions about the laws of physics.[33] More specifically, it does not require us to suppose that those laws are strict, or deterministic. Suppositions about the strictness of physical laws may create their own problems, but the problem that we are encountering here is one that arises without them. Our present problem persists, even if the laws of nature are ones in which randomness plays a part.

That is because the idea that creates our problem is just the idea that all of the facts about the properties of the world *at any time* are settled by the world's physical properties *at that particular time*. This idea is hard to deny, whatever you think about the laws of nature that figure in the world's underlying physics. The score on some dice at a particular time is settled by the physical configuration, *at that time*, of the dots on their upper faces. This score is settled *now*, by the present configuration of the dots, whether or not the process of rolling the dice involved physical laws that were strict or chancy.[34] If the present facts about one's mind are settled by the present facts about one's brain (much as the present facts about the score are settled by the present facts about the dots), and if these facts about one's brain are governed only by the laws of physics (whether or not those laws are deterministic), then one's mental states seem to be superfluous to any of the causal processes in which they had seemed to play a role.

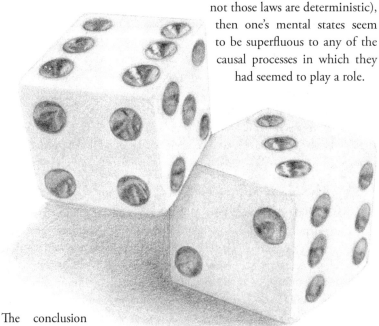

The conclusion to which this line of thought seems to lead is that, although our mental states appear to interact with one another, and with other things, this is a mere appearance: Much as the shadow of a bat might appear to interact with the shadow of a ball, the real causal interactions are elsewhere. The movement of the bat's shadow makes no genuine contribution to the trajectory of the ball's shadow. The worry that we are facing is that our beliefs, hopes, and moods, are similarly unable to make any real contribution to the trajectory of our lives. It is the worry that, when we consider these mental occurrences, we are only ever seeing mental shadows of chemical and physical processes.

That conclusion would create a problem for the approach to mental disorder at which we arrived some pages ago, according to which the mental disorders are those disorders to the manifestation or development of which mental events make an ongoing causal contribution. If everything that is required for the causation of mental events occurs at the chemical and physical levels, then this includes everything that is required for the causation of those mental events that figure in the experience of mental disorder. The line of thought that we have just considered therefore suggests that physics and chemistry allow no room for there to be any genuinely mental disorders, in the sense of mental disorder that we have identified. Just as hyperthyroidism might seem to its sufferer to be a mental disorder, when in fact the problem is a bodily one, so it can begin to seem that every other disorder that we currently take to be mental must in fact have a bodily origin, albeit one that we currently know little about.

The problem created by this line of thought is a pressing one, and our preferred account of mental disorders is not the only thing that is threatened by it. This problematic line of thought threatens our whole understanding of the reasons for our thoughts and feelings. It is this – and not some local problem in the definition of mental disorders – that makes the line of thought so bothersome.

The understanding that comes under threat here is crucial to our common-sense picture of ourselves. That common-sense picture is one in which we can be happy, and can know it. We can, as a result, clap our hands. The happiness and the clapping would seem to be related as cause and effect, but in the light of the ideas that we have just been considering, it is

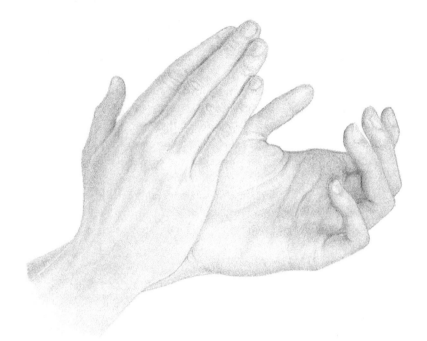

difficult to see how this could possibly be so. Were we to inspect the events that triggered the muscular contractions through which our hand-clapping is coordinated, we would find nothing but nerve cells firing, and neurotransmitters being released. Some features of these nerve cells and neurotransmitters must have something to do with the happiness that we feel, but it seems only to be their biochemical properties that figure in the laws of nature by which their causal interactions are governed. It therefore seems to be these biochemical properties that do all of the causal and explanatory work. If we are to avoid giving up on this common-sense picture, by saying that nobody knows the real reasons for their actions unless they know about the underlying chemistry of their brain, then we need to face some difficult questions about the way in which the causal explanations of human behavior operate.

The mystery surrounding these questions is deepened by their reputation for philosophical obscurity. We try to cast some light on them in the concluding sections of this book.

# Notes to Chapter 1.2

26    Here again our approach parallels that taken by George Graham in the opening chapters of his useful 2013 textbook, *The Disordered Mind* (Routledge).

The two-step approach that we have taken may seem uncontroversial, but in order to justify its adoption some substantial assumptions are needed. Adopting it is not a purely pragmatic matter. That is because, for the purposes of analyzing the reference of any noun-phrase that is composed from an adjective and a noun – any phrase like "mental disorder," or "partial attention," or "fake gun" – it may not always be a good idea to analyze the noun and the adjective separately. If you want to understand what fake guns are, you should not ask what makes them guns, and then – as a separate piece of explanatory business – ask what makes them fake. If you want to understand what the mental disorders are, it may or may not be a good idea to ask what makes them disorders, and then to ask – as a separate piece of explanatory business – what it is that makes them mental.

27    The idea that mental disorders are all and only those disorders with mental symptoms is perhaps too simplistic for anyone actually to have believed it. The idea is nonetheless present in the background of some discussions, as if it were a natural thing to think. The idea can, for example, be seen in Edward Dolnick's 1998 book, *Madness on the Couch: Blaming the Victim in the Heyday of Psychoanalysis* (Simon and Schuster).

28    Our emphasis on sustaining causes, rather than triggering causes, picks up a suggestion that is made by Bernard Gert and Charles M. Culver in "Defining mental disorder," published in 2004 as Chapter 29 of *The Philosophy of Psychiatry: A Companion,* edited by Jennifer Radden (Oxford University Press) 415–425.

Radden herself elaborates a version of this idea in her 2007 paper "Epidemic depression and Burtonian melancholy," a paper that was first published in *Philosophical Papers* 36, no. 3 (2007): 443–464, and subsequently reprinted as Chapter 6 of her 2009 book, *Moody Minds Distempered* (Oxford University Press).

29    For an account of how differences between mental processes and bodily processes lead to some clear distinctions between mental disorders and physical disorders, see Nomy Arpaly's article "How it is not 'Just like diabetes': Mental disorders and the moral psychologist." *Philosophical Issues* 15, no. 1 (2005): 282–298.

30    Those outside of philosophy are sometimes surprised to learn how many difficulties philosophers have found there to be in the everyday notion of one event causing another. Aristotle, in his *Metaphysics,* distinguished between four different notions of "cause," and the idea that at least one of these ancient notions might be spurious has been a guiding insight for much scientific thinking, throughout the renaissance and also more recently, in debates about quantum mechanics. The modern tradition of puzzlement about what causation is, and about how it should be fitted into our picture of the world, begins with the work of David Hume, in his 1748 *An Enquiry Concerning Human Understanding.* Some of the more recent philosophical thinking on this topic is represented in the papers that are collected by Huw Price and Richard Corry in their 2006 volume, *Causation, Physics, and the Constitution of Reality: Russell's Republic Revisited* (Oxford University Press).

Philosophical discussions of causation have tended to focus, for the sake of simplicity, on cases in which one event produces another subsequent event, rather as the motion of the cue ball causes the motion of an object ball on the billiard table. Such cases are easy to picture (and Hume himself was a man who enjoyed a game of billiards), but more recent work has emphasized the ways in which this simple picture might be misleading, especially when we come to consider systems with the complexity of the human brain. Philosophical work examining the need, in neuroscience, for a picture of causation that is more network-like, and less linear, can be found in Carl F. Craver's 2007 book, *Explaining the Brain: Mechanisms and the Mosaic Unity of Neuroscience* (Oxford University Press). In his 2003 book, *Making Things Happen: A Theory of Causal Explanation* (Oxford University Press), James Woodward has developed a particular theoretical framework within which more complex causal interactions can be understood. He relates this to some of the issues about mental causation, such as those that we consider here, in a 2008 paper, "Mental causation and neural mechanisms." The paper is published in Jakob Hohwy and Jesper Kallestrup (eds.), *Being Reduced: New Essays on Reduction, Explanation, and Causation* (Oxford University Press).

31    The problem that we are facing here is the psychiatric version of a problem that is known to philosophers as the causal exclusion problem. That problem received an influential treatment in Jaegwon Kim's 1998 book *Mind in a Physical World: An Essay on the Mind-Body Problem and Mental Causation.* (MIT Press). It has been discussed from a variety of perspectives, many of which are represented in a 2013 volume, *Mental Causation and Ontology,* edited by Sophie C. Gibb, Rögnvaldur Ingthorsson, and E. Jonathan Lowe (Oxford University Press).

Stephen Yablo's papers "Mental causation," *Philosophical Review* 101, no. 2 (1992): 245–280, and "Causal relevance," *Philosophical Issues* 13, no. 1(2003): 316–328, are both highlights of the recent literature. They suggest a promising line by which the causal exclusion problem might be solved. Both are reprinted in the first volume of Yablo's collected papers, *Thoughts* (Oxford University Press, 2008). The argument that we develop in this book's final chapter follows the outline of Yablo's (although our presentation takes a somewhat cavalier attitude to points that Yablo treats with far more precision).

32     The problem about free will – which is not the problem under discussion here – is one of the more provocative problems in the philosophy of mind. A very good discussion of it can be found in Daniel C. Dennett's 1984 book *Elbow Room: The Varieties of Free Will Worth Wanting* (MIT Press). A range of perspectives on the topic are represented in *Four Views on Free Will*, a 2007 book that was severally authored by John Martin Fischer, Robert Kane, Derk Pereboom, and Manuel Vargas (Blackwell Publishing).

33     The particular problem about free will that arises in connection with deterministic physics has received an influential treatment in Peter van Inwagen's 1983 book, *An Essay on Free Will* (Oxford University Press), and in a number of van Inwagen's related papers.

34     Although the introduction of jargon is not, in general, a source of philosophical perspicuity, the vocabulary that has been introduced in discussions of the point that we are concerned with here is sometimes useful to know when reading the philosophical literature. If we frame it in such jargon then the point that we are making here is that the problem of causal exclusion arises from the strictness of the mind's *supervenience on* the physical, and not from the strictness of the causal relations between physical events. The term "supervenience" is defined so that the claim that X-facts (e.g., facts about the mind) *supervene* on Y-facts (e.g., facts about the brain) means that it would be impossible for there to be two situations that are the same, with regard to the Y-facts that are true in those situations, but that are different with regard to the X-facts that are true in them. Terence Horgan provides a comprehensive survey of the strengths and weaknesses of this notion in his 1993 paper, "From supervenience to superdupervenience: Meeting the demands of a material world." *Mind* 102, no. 408 (1993): 555–586.

# 1.3 What Makes a Mental Disorder *Disordered*?

We have outlined an answer to our first question – "what makes some disorder qualify as *mental*?" – and have seen that the attempt to make sense of that answer leads immediately into a philosophical conundrum, concerning the possibility of mental causation. We have presented that conundrum, but have not yet attempted to answer it. Even with these accompanying complexities, our first question is less fraught than our second, which is: "What makes some mental condition qualify as *disordered*?"

These two questions are fraught in different ways. Our first question was difficult because it led to a challenge for our understanding of mental causation (and so led to a challenge for our common-sense understanding of ourselves, as people who can take decisions, and who can act for reasons). Our second question is difficult because it involves something like an appraisal. Its difficulties are to do with value.[35]

As with many questions that are to do with value, answering this second question requires a balance to be struck. We should prefer not to be diagnosing mental disorder where there is none – where there is, instead, only diversity, or difference, or the less lovely aspects of a normal human life.[36] We should prefer not to be saying that people have mental disorders if they are distressed only because they are coping normally with some disturbing circumstances. We should also prefer not to say that they are suffering from a disorder if they are instead facing the psychological consequences of their own laziness, or recklessness, or rudeness.

We therefore need to avoid applying diagnoses where they do not belong, but there is also a risk of injustice if we withhold diagnoses in cases where they ought properly to be applied. Over the course of the twentieth century, a great many people were liberated from accusations of laziness, of stupidity,[37] and even of demonic possession,[38] by such diagnoses as Depression, Dyslexia,[39] and Dissociative fugue. Our understanding of these particular conditions was, at that time, a work in progress, and our current diagnostic practices handle these conditions rather differently. The liberating work that these diagnoses accomplished did not need to be postponed until our understanding of them had stabilized.

If we give a wrong answer to the question of what qualifies some mental condition as disordered then we risk doing one sort of injustice to the people who are diagnosed, and we risk doing another sort of injustice to those from whom a diagnosis is withheld. We also risk injustices if, finding this question to be difficult, we demur from answering it until some further progress in the science of psychiatry has been made. The curative mission that is at the heart of medicine often demands that we act with imperfect knowledge, to do the best we can to help the patient who is in front of us now.

If our answer to this chapter's question is to avoid doing any of these injustices, it seems obvious that it should take account of the distress, and of the deficits, that are experienced by those persons who exhibit the conditions that we judge to be disorderly. But it should be equally obvious that such distress cannot be the whole of our reason for classifying some person's condition as a disordered one. Distress may, in some cases, be a salutary response. It may be a perfectly normal reaction to being abandoned, or to being imperilled.

It is not only distress, but also *deficiency*, that has a place in normal life. Everyone, after all, is likely to be abnormally bad at something. Deficiency should not by itself be thought to give sufficient grounds for taking some condition to be a diagnosable disorder, even if this deficiency is one that psychiatry would be equipped to alleviate. The deficiencies in a mediocre chess player's endgame might perhaps be alleviated by a dose of attention-enhancing drugs, of the sort that psychiatrists prescribe routinely. But, even if this chess player's failings cause her genuine distress, we do not want to find ourselves in the position of saying that her lack of endgame mastery is a mental disorder. Not every deficit is a disorder, not even if it is a distressing mental deficit, and not even if it is a deficit that would be treatable by psychiatric means.

Nor is every mental disorder distressing – at least not for the person whose mental condition is disordered. We can see this by considering Narcissistic personality disorder.[40] People with this disorder have a grandiose sense of their own importance. They believe themselves to be worthy of special consideration by others. According to the fifth edition of the American Psychiatric Association's *Diagnostic and Statistical Manual of Mental Disorders*, persons with Narcissistic personality disorder are preoccupied with the idea of their own "unlimited success, power, brilliance, beauty, or ideal love."[41]

This condition is classified as a mental disorder, even when distress plays no notable role in the mental life of the person experiencing it.[42] Since mental disorders may not be distressing for their sufferers, and since some distressing mental deficits are *not* disorders, we need to find some notion of disorder that does not equate disorder with distress.

We might hope to find such a notion by instead equating disorder with *malfunctioning*.[43] This would be a natural accompaniment to the attitude that treats psychiatry as being on a par with the other branches of medicine. In those other branches of medicine, disorderliness can often be identified whenever there is an occurrence of malfunctioning, whether or not this malfunctioning leads to distress.

We see an example of this in the liver condition that is known as "Gilbert's syndrome." The livers of people with Gilbert's syndrome metabolize bilirubin in an abnormal way (resulting from the reduced activity of a specific enzyme). They therefore have an unusually high concentration of unconjugated bilirubin in their bloodstream. Most of these people suffer no ill effects from their condition, but the condition is, nonetheless, a result of malfunctioning, and it is therefore recognized by hepatology as a disorder that is worth identifying.

If the hepatologist can understand liver disorder as being a malfunctioning of the liver, whether or not this malfunction causes any distress on the part of that liver's owner, then perhaps we could equally well understand mental disorder as being a malfunctioning of the mind, whether or not this causes any distress to the person whose mind it is. We could then say that the person with Narcissistic personality disorder has a genuine disorder, even if he suffers no distress as a result of it. We could say this on the grounds that his processes of self-appraisal are failing to function in a proper way. We would also be able to say that the struggling chess player has *no* disorder, even if her distress is genuine, since her mental processes are performing all of their normal functions successfully, despite the fact that those functions are not sufficient to secure the victories that this chess player desires.

Because it enables us to give the right answer when considering the otherwise difficult cases of Narcissistic personality disorder and unsuccessful chess playing, this introduction of the concept of "malfunctioning" would seem to be a step that takes us in the right direction, but it is not a step that takes us very far unless we also have some concept of *proper* functioning.[44] Without such a concept, the worry is that we have merely replaced the word "disorder" with the word "malfunction," without thereby throwing any light on our question of what it is that makes a mental disorder *disordered*.

The limitations of introducing this concept of malfunction to our account of disorder mark one of the ways in which psychiatry faces complications that go beyond the complications faced by other branches of medicine. So long as we are considering those other branches of medicine, it seems that concepts of proper functioning and malfunctioning can be derived from biology. A liver's processing of bilirubin can then be counted as being a part of its proper functioning because the failure to process bilirubin would lead to a breakdown, or at least to a deterioration, in something that is biologically necessary. It could, for example, lead to pathological jaundice.

This notion of biological function may be clear enough when we apply it to the liver[45] (although even here there is room for controversy).[46] It would, however, be of limited use for understanding the functions of the mind, and of the brain. That is because the consequences of disruptions to the normal activities of a mind may not have any direct effect on processes that are *biologically* necessary.

It has sometimes been suggested that a more adequate conception of "proper functioning" can be supplied by evolution, so that the proper function of a thing should be understood as being that function for which it evolved.[47] The thought here would be that those of our ancestors who did well in the struggle for survival did so, in part, on account of the efficiency with which they could process bilirubin, with the result that the liver's production of bilirubin can be counted as part of its proper functioning, whereas the liver's higher levels of unconjugated bilirubin in Gilbert's syndrome can be counted as being outside the norms of proper functioning, because these made no contribution to our ancestors' survival.[48]

This notion of normal functioning may indeed play a role in biology. When it is said that the function of a gallbladder is to store bile, for example, it seems to be this notion that is being employed. It nonetheless seems that in the context of medicine, and especially in the context of psychiatric medicine, this notion of proper functioning cannot do the work that is needed.[49]

It would not in general be true to say that medicine looks to evolution to tell it when some organ is functioning correctly. Doing so in the psychiatric case would give entirely the wrong results. Although benefitting from the fruits of evolution can maximize the likelihood that you will survive and reproduce – and so can maximize the chances that livers will produce an amount of bilirubin that is optimal for supporting life – the process of evolution is necessarily indifferent to those aspects of your psychology that would have done nothing to propagate your genes in the brutal and preliterate world where humans evolved. Some of our ancestors successfully propagated their genes on account of being cruel, ruthless, and promiscuous.[50] Insofar as their brains promoted such behavior, those brains may have contributed to their evolutionary success. But a mind that fails to sustain cruel and ruthless promiscuity is not thereby malfunctioning, and a mind that is doing something other than the things for which it evolved is not, on that account, disordered.

In the psychiatric case we are therefore left without an evolutionary grounding for our concept of *proper* functions, and so we are left without any evolutionary basis on which to construct an answer, independent of relatively recent social systems and their mores, to our question of what it is for a brain or mind to be *malfunctioning*.

Although we have seen that neither biology nor a person's own experience of distress sets a standard of functioning relative to which the mental disorders are shown to be instances of malfunctioning, we can continue to look for conceptions of functioning and malfunctioning, without turning our backs on biological functions, or on experiences of distress. We can instead allow our standards of malfunctioning to be set by some combination of biological factors, experiences of distress, and sundry other things. The standards relative to which a patient's mental life has gone wrong can then be understood as being the broadly defined standards of a flourishing human – this being one who has the capacity to accomplish any of the various things that humans normally do accomplish, when their lives are going well.

The American Psychiatric Association employs something like these broad standards of what mental health requires, and so of what mental disorder involves, when it specifies, for most of the disorders that it identifies, that these can be diagnosed only if "the disturbance causes clinically significant distress or impairment in social, occupational, or other important areas of functioning."[51]

If we had a sense of what it is for some distress or impairment to be "clinically significant," and of what it is for an "area of functioning" to be "important," then this official formula could tell us what it is that makes a mental disorder disordered. But on both of these questions there is room for opinions to differ, and there is reason to suppose that they will in fact differ in all of the difficult cases: The person with Narcissistic personality disorder might disagree with those people who have to work with him on the question of whether the disruptions caused by his self-importance are "clinically significant"; the failing chess player may differ from her family on the question of whether the arena of chess is an "important area of functioning." When determining what it is for some area of functioning to be important, we should prefer not to impose our opinions on those who don't share them. This is just the sort of difficulty that we had been hoping to avoid.

The American Psychiatric Association's diagnostic formula therefore skirts our difficult second question. There may be good reasons for wanting to skirt it, but there are crucial issues that remain unresolved if we do so.

In this section we have said that, whereas the liver's proper functioning may be determined by its physiological characteristics, or by the history of its evolution, a more general criterion for human flourishing would need to be many faceted. In saying this, we can acknowledge that those mental conditions that might threaten a person's flourishing can take quite various forms. And saying this opens up a new set of philosophical questions.

The many facets to our conception of flourishing mean that, in our conception of a healthy mind, various social and cultural factors will need to be taken into account. Because humans are social beings – because we are, as Aristotle said, "a political animal"[52] – our interactions with the structures of a society feature in the conduct of our lives, and so contribute to the possibility of those lives going well. Disorderly social interactions can therefore threaten our opportunities for flourishing.

From the need to take account of these social factors, psychiatry inherits a wealth of complications, relating to the various ways in which the structures of a society provide the context in which our well-being must be achieved.[53] It should therefore be no surprise that many theorists of mental disorder over the last century – from Freud, to Fanon, to Foucault[54] – have also been concerned with broader questions about societies, about cultures, and about the various orderly and disorderly ways in which we find our places in them. Part Two of this book considers some of those questions.

# Notes to Chapter 1.3

35    In moving from our first question to our second, we are moving between two of the major branches of philosophical enquiry. Our first question
belonged to the branch of philosophy that is concerned with *metaphysics*. The
issues connected with it were issues about *what there is*, and about the ways in
which things behave. Our second questions belong to the branch of philosophy
that is concerned with *value theory*, or *axiology*. The issues here are connected
with the matter of why and when there are things that *ought to be* some way.

36    The complaint that psychiatric diagnoses regard aspects of normal life
as if they were medical disorders is elaborated by Allan V. Horwitz and Jerome
C. Wakefield in their 2007 book, *The Loss of Sadness: How Psychiatry Trans-
formed Normal Sorrow into Depressive Disorder* (Oxford University Press), and by
Peter Conrad in his 2008 *The Medicalization of Society: On the Transformation of
Human Conditions into Treatable Disorders* (Johns Hopkins University Press).

37    Peter Byrne provides a brief but wide-ranging account of the ways
in which stereotypes operate in the media's representation of psychiatry, in his
1997 article: "Psychiatric stigma: Past, passing and to come." *Journal of the Royal
Society of Medicine* 90, no. 11 (1997): 618–621. Byrne is careful to articulate
the ways in which stereotypes shape the discourse about psychiatrists themselves, as well as the discourse about their patients.

38    It is a commonplace, in discussions of mental illness, that some of
the conditions that are now diagnosed as psychiatric disorders would previously
have been attributed to the influence of nefarious supernatural forces. Simon
Kemp and Kevin Williams review the evidence for this, with reference to a
range of cultural settings, in an article entitled "Demonic possession and mental
disorder in medieval and early modern Europe." *Psychological Medicine* 17, no.
1 (1987): 21–29.

39    Barbara Riddick combines individual case histories and population-level statistics in order to explore the significance of the diagnosis of Dyslexia in her 1996 book, *Living with Dyslexia: The Social and Emotional Consequences of Specific Learning Difficulties/Disabilities* (Routledge).

40    The depiction of Narcissus on p. 38 is a study of a detail from John
William Waterhouse's 1903 painting *Echo and Narcissus*.

41    The full set of diagnostic criteria for Narcissistic personality disorder
can be found on page 669 of the DSM-5.

42     People with higher levels of narcissism (but with levels of the trait that nonetheless fall short of those seen in Narcissistic personality disorder) may show less loneliness, and more subjective well-being, than people without narcissistic traits.  Evidence for this is shown by Constantine Sedikides, Eric A. Rudich, Aiden P. Gregg, Madoka Kumashiro, and Caryl Rusbult, in their 2004 paper "Are normal narcissists psychologically healthy?: Self-esteem matters." *Journal of Personality and Social Psychology* 87, no. 3 (2004): 400–416.

Those people who have levels of narcissism that *are* sufficient for a diagnosis of Narcissistic personality disorder present a more complicated picture, and they do, in some cases, show distress, despite their high opinion of their own significance.  Discussion of this can be found in Joshua D. Miller, W. Keith Campbell, and Paul A. Pilkonis, "Narcissistic personality disorder: Relations with distress and functional impairment." *Comprehensive Psychiatry* 48, no. 2 (2007): 170–177.

43     There is a long history of discussions concerning the idea that disease and disorder stand in some sort of essential relationship to *malfunctioning*. Christopher Megone identifies that idea's Aristotelian roots in his article, "Mental illness, human function, and values." *Philosophy, Psychiatry & Psychology* 7, no. 1 (2000): 45–65.

44     Tim Thornton argues against the idea that claims about proper function can provide a route via which the evaluative aspects of psychiatric diagnosis can be reduced to merely descriptive claims about biology.  His argument can be found in a 2000 paper, "Mental illness and reductionism: Can functions be naturalized?" *Philosophy, Psychiatry & Psychology* 7, no. 1 (2000): 67–76. Thornton's paper also places these ideas into the context of some broader debates about naturalism and reductionism.

45     The liver depicted on p. 79 is a study drawn from a 1903 lithograph, *Human Internal Organs*.

46     The difficulties in explicating the biological notion of "function" were examined by Peter Achinstein in his 1977 paper "Function statements." *Philosophy of Science* 44, no. 3 (1977): 341–367.  The range of these difficulties, and some possible solutions to them, are discussed in the papers collected by André Ariew, Robert Cummins, and Mark Perlman, in an edited volume from 2002: *Functions: New Essays in the Philosophy of Psychology and Biology* (Oxford University Press).

47     The idea that psychiatry should be "based on an evolutionary understanding of disorders" is explored by Luc Faucher in his 2016 paper, "Darwinian

blues: Evolutionary psychiatry and depression," published in Jerome C. Wakefield and Steeves Demazeux (eds.) *Sadness or Depression?: International Perspectives on the Depression Epidemic and Its Meaning* (Springer).

Jerome C. Wakefield's own work sets out one way in which evolution might be used to provide psychiatry with a notion of function and dysfunction. Some examples of his thinking on this topic can be seen in a 1992 article "The concept of mental disorder: On the boundary between biological facts and social values" *American Psychologist* 47, no. 3 (1992): 373–388, and again in a 1999 article, "Evolutionary versus prototype analysis of the concept of disorder" *Journal of Abnormal Psychology* 108, no. 3 (1999): 374–399.

48    It is assumed, in giving this evolutionary explanation for the disorderliness of Gilbert's syndrome, that the level of unconjugated bilirubin found in most people is the level that is most biologically fit. But although Gilbert's syndrome is associated with an increased risk of some other disorders (such as gallstones), it has recently been postulated that Gilbert's syndrome may in fact be associated with a *decrease* in all-cause mortality. The association with reproductive fitness remains unknown. A discussion of the relevant evidence can be found in Laura J. Horsfall, Irwin Nazareth, Stephen P. Pereira, and Irene Petersen's 2013, "Gilbert's syndrome and the risk of death: A population-based cohort study." *Journal of Gastroenterology and Hepatology* 28, no. 10 (2013): 1643–1647.

49    For general objections to the idea that there is a role in medical thinking for an evolution-based concept of normal function, see Ron Amundson's paper, "Against normal function." *Studies in History and Philosophy of Science Part C: Studies in History and Philosophy of Biological and Biomedical Sciences* 31, no. 1 (200): 33–53.

50    Evolutionary explanations of dysfunctional traits (such as cruelty, ruthlessness, and promiscuity) are discussed by David M. Buss and Todd K. Shackelford in their article "Human aggression in evolutionary psychological perspective." *Clinical Psychology Review* 17, no. 6 (1997): 605–619. Questions about the role of evolutionary explanations in psychology more generally have, for some years, been hotly debated. In their paper, "Evolutionary psychology: A view from evolutionary biology" *Psychological Inquiry* 13, no. 2 (2002): 150–156, Elisabeth A. Lloyd and Marcus Feldman argue against many of the assumptions on which they claim evolutionary psychology depends. Edouard Machery mounts a defense of some lines of evolutionary psychology in "Discovery and confirmation in evolutionary psychology", his contribution to the forthcoming *Oxford Handbook of the Philosophy of Psychology* (Oxford University Press). Philip Gerrans relates some of the issues here to questions about mental

disorder in his 2007 paper "Mechanisms of madness: Evolutionary psychiatry without evolutionary psychology." *Biology and Philosophy* 22, no. 1: 35–56.

51     Critical discussion of the DSM's general criterion for clinical significance can be found in Robert L. Spitzer and Jerome C. Wakefield's 1999 article, "DSM-IV diagnostic criterion for clinical significance: Does it help solve the false positives problem?" *American Journal of Psychiatry* 156, no. 12 (1999): 1856–1864.

52     It is in the *Nicomachean Ethics* that Aristotle makes his famous remarks about humans being, by nature, political. This notion of "political animals" is introduced in Aristotle's history of animals, as applying not only to humans but also to social insects such as bees and ants, and to other creatures that naturally dwell together in cooperative groups.

53     In this chapter we have been assuming that it is the job of psychiatry to remove certain impediments to human flourishing, and have been trying to explain what this flourishing amounts to. A conception of human flourishing based only on distress was shown to be inadequate for this role, as was a conception based only on biological functioning, or based only on criteria that were set with reference to evolutionary considerations. We have therefore suggested that these notions should be supplemented with conceptions that have their basis in facts about the societies and cultures within which our flourishing needs to be achieved. (We have also admitted that this introduces complications, the discussion of which is postponed until the next section.)

Our claim here is only that social factors must make some contribution to the standards of human flourishing, alongside factors that are rooted in biology, and factors that are rooted in first-person experiences of well-being or distress. Our claim is not that social factors are *always* central to diagnosis. In order to understand why the experiences of a particular depressed or anxious person are a case of disorder, it may in some cases be of little explanatory use to mention the social context of those experiences.

54     In several of his works – and especially in his 1913 *Totem und Tabu: Einige Übereinstimmungen im Seelenleben der Wilden und der Neurotiker* (published in English, in the Vintage edition of Freud's Complete Works, as *Totem and Taboo*) – Sigmund Freud's thinking frequently moved between the theorizing of mental disorder, and its treatment, and the theorizing of anthropology. He is portrayed on p. 41.

The prevailing theoretical flow in the work of Frantz Fanon (who is portrayed on p. 42) runs in the opposite direction. His 1952 book, *Peau noire, masques blancs* (*Black Skin, White Masks* (Pluto Press)), and his 1961 *Les damnés de la terre* (*The Wretched of the Earth* (Grove Press)) both draw on his expertise in psychiatry, in order to theorize the experience of colonialism.

Michel Foucault's career also begins with psychiatry and moves from there into a more wide-ranging sociological position, of an increasingly ambitious scope. Foucault's 1961 *Folie et déraison: histoire de la folie à l'âge classique* (*Madness and Civilization* (Routledge)) considers the way in which a society's conception of mental disorder reflects other aspects of that society's conception of the individual. A great deal of relevant thinking can also be found in Foucault's (1963) *Naissance de la clinique* (*The Birth of the Clinic* (Pantheon Books)), and in his vast *Histoire de la sexualité*, published in four volumes from 1976 to 2018 (*The History of Sexuality* (Vintage)). His portrait is shown on p. 43.

# Part Two: Psychiatry and Society

# Outline of Part Two

## 2.1 Two Ways in Which Social Factors Can Contribute to Mental Disorder

Some of the social factors contributing to human flourishing are large-scale cultural phenomena. Others are more local facts, concerning individual relationships. This creates a methodological challenge, since it is hard to bring large and small factors into focus at the same time. We do need to bring both into focus, since both can contribute to mental disorders, and to bodily ones. We can distinguish between two different forms that these contributions take. The first is that of contributing causally to the bringing about of some condition. The second is that of contributing, not to the fact that the condition occurs, but to the fact that it constitutes an impediment to human flourishing. We illustrate this second sort of contribution, in the bodily case, by considering the way in which social factors contribute to the unpleasantness, but not to the causation, of having a facial birthmark. We illustrate it in the mental case by considering the tics that are characteristic of Tourette's disorder. The cases of Attention deficit hyperactivity disorder and Autism spectrum disorder show how these two sorts of contribution can become entangled.

## 2.2 Are We Changing People When We Should Be Changing Societies?

Since social factors play a role in the conception of human flourishing with which psychiatry operates, a question arises about whether psychiatry serves to enforce merely social norms. Psychiatry has often been criticized on these grounds. Care must be taken to ensure that the authority of psychiatry is not used oppressively, but attempts to reject all psychiatry as oppressive should be treated with suspicion, as should attempts to exonerate the entire field. Individual cases must be considered on their own merits. In cases of Tourette's disorder and cases of delusion, we show that psychiatric practice need not be coercive or oppressive. But, in these cases and in others, mental well-being may best be served by making changes that maximize the social opportunities for flourishing, and not by exclusively focussing on ways in which individuals can be brought in line with the demands of society's status quo. Psychiatry can play a role in changes of both sorts.

## 2.3 Sexuality and Disobedience

The previous chapter argued that care needs to be taken, on a case-by-case basis, to ensure that psychiatric practice is not coercive or oppressive. This chapter considers some of the cases that pose particular difficulties. It is shown, in the case of Oppositional defiant disorder, that political considerations must play a role in determining whether a diagnosis is appropriate. This diagnosis cannot be value-free. And in the case of disorders involving sexuality our diagnostic practices can be seen to have changed, in ways that reflect changes in our society's conception of the role that is played by sexuality in the life of a flourishing human. In the particular case of homosexuality, these changes to our social conception of flourishing are on their way to becoming properly established. In other cases, such as those involving cross-dressing, hypo-sexuality, and voyeurism, there are ongoing debates, in which several different values are in contention. Since the appropriateness of its diagnostic scheme depends on the values that are recognized by the society within which it operates, psychiatry cannot extricate itself from the complexity of these debates.

## 2.1 Two Ways in Which Social Factors Can Contribute to Mental Disorder

Because humans flourish in a social context, our achievement of flourishing depends upon our interactions with the societies in which we find ourselves.[55] Things taking place on either side of these interactions can jeopardize their success, and thereby contribute to the disordering of a life. They can therefore play a role in the disordering of a mind. When we are looking to give an explanation for such disordering, the contributions that are made by social factors may be just as important as the contributions that we make ourselves. Psychiatrists therefore need to consider the ways in which people interact socially, in addition to considering those people as individuals. Although psychiatric practice often aspires to being "patient centered," it should never be so exclusively focussed on its patients that their social contexts fade entirely into the background.

The social contributors to a mental disorder might take several forms. They might take the form of relationships with particular people, who might be individual family members,[56] romantic partners,[57] or social peers.[58] They might also take the form of relationships to broader social phenomena, such as the attitudes and values that are, for better or worse, embodied in our culture.[59] A mental disorder might be triggered by the disordering of one's individual relationships, or by the disordering of one's relationship to these broader social factors (or by something altogether different). Particular and general social factors might also contribute to the maintenance of a disorder, without being its initial trigger.

These different sorts of social contribution might operate separately, and so might pull in various directions. They might support one another, as seems to happen in some cases of eating disorders, when particular relationships and broader social mores conspire to reinforce the hopes and habits that cause a person's eating to become problematic.[60] They might also pull in opposite directions, as seems to happen in some cases of Substance use disorder, when some social relationships might reinforce the use of a substance, and others might discourage it.[61] This opposition of forces might result in an equilibrium. It might also result in something that is more like turmoil.

Because the social contributors to mental disorder are so diverse, and because the methods needed to study them demand quite different pieces of expertise, it can be difficult to find a theoretical perspective from which to view all of the social factors that are relevant to the development and maintenance of any one disorder, together with all of the factors that are relevant to the way in which that disorder might spread through a population. The finding of such a perspective might nonetheless be necessary, if we are to keep sight of everything that is explanatorily important.

Our explanations of mental disorder are unlikely to be complete if we focus exclusively on the broader influences of culture, or if we focus exclusively on the particular influences of individual relationships. Theories that talk *only* about the influence of a patriarchal society are no more likely to be complete than are the theories that talk *only* about the consequences of an insecure attachment to one's mother. Psychiatrists have been rightly suspicious of an academic culture in which a particular type of theory becomes the defining tenet by which one discipline distinguishes itself from another. Rather than deciding which of these local theories is the most important, we instead need to understand the ways in which they might operate together.[62]

We can distinguish between two quite different sorts of social contribution, whether we are considering bodily disorders or mental ones.[63] Social factors might, on the one hand, contribute to causing the occurrence of a condition (either by helping to trigger it, or by helping to maintain it). On the other hand, they might contribute to the fact that a condition is disorderly.

It is worth taking a moment to be clear about what this second sort of contribution amounts to. We can bring it to light by seeing how the distinction between these two sorts of contribution operates in the bodily case, where it is relatively clear, and then applying it to the mental case, where it is rather more subtle.

Starting, then, with bodily disorders, we can see a social contribution of this second sort by considering the example of someone who has a vascular birthmark on their face. Social factors make no causal contribution to the occurrence of such birthmarks. Their cause is entirely a matter of vascular abnormality. But it is clear that social factors do contribute to the way in which the presence of a birthmark might bring distress into one's life. The most significant impairment will, in many cases, be the impact that this vascular abnormality has on social interactions. Social factors make no contribution to the occurrence of this condition, but do contribute to the extent to which the condition is disorderly for the person who has it.

Lung cancer provides an example of the opposite sort. Social factors do contribute causally to the occurrence of lung cancer – by increasing the likelihood that one will be exposed, in various ways, to carcinogens – but in this case it is clear that no social contribution is needed in order to explain the fact that a cancerous lung is a disorderly thing to have.

In the case of a vascular birthmark, social factors contribute to the extent of the condition's disorderliness. In the case of lung cancer they make a contribution to the likelihood of the condition's occurrence. The cancer case is one in which social factors help to make something happen, but do not explain why that thing is disorderly. The birthmark case is one in which social factors do not make the thing happen, but do contribute to the extent of that thing's being disorderly.

In these bodily cases the two sorts of contribution are clearly different, and operate by quite different mechanisms. The distinction between these two sorts of contribution can still be drawn when we move from considering bodily cases to considering mental ones, but, in most actual cases of mental disorder, it will be easy for the two sorts of contribution to become entangled.

An example of this entanglement can be seen by considering the tics that are symptomatic of Tourette's disorder. These tics are often small and repeated movements of the body or the face, such as eye-blinking or shoulder shrugging. In some cases – leaving out those instances of the disorder in which tics cause self-injury, or impede communication – the propensity to tic might not be especially upsetting, when considered in itself. It might nonetheless be a disruption to one's flourishing, on account of the way in which it affects social interactions. Tourettic tics can be thought of, in these cases, as being somewhat analogous to the case of a facial birthmark: the disorder can be thought of as a case in which social factors are making a contribution to the fact that some condition is disorderly.

And yet the contribution of social factors will not only be of that sort: the patient's awareness of this socially mediated disorderliness might also increase the likelihood of his tics occurring, and so it might make a contribution of the other sort, by making a causal contribution to the triggering and maintenance of those tics.[64] In this way, the two sorts of social influence can become entangled.

Tourette's disorder is unusual in being a mental condition in which the principal symptom has an overt bodily manifestation. It might therefore seem to be an unrepresentative example with which to illustrate the distinction with which we are presently concerned, but a similar point could be made about mental disorders in which the symptoms are less conspicuously on display. Like facial birthmarks, and like the bodily tics of a patient with Tourette's disorder, some of the reasoning patterns that are characteristic of Autism spectrum disorder might be detrimental to flourishing only because of the ways in which they impair interaction in normal social contexts. Those reasoning patterns need not be disorderly in themselves.[65] Sometimes they might even be advantageous.[66] And here again the two sorts of social contribution are likely to become entangled: the social facts that make autistic symptoms disorderly may also contribute causally to the occurence of those symptoms.

Something similar can be said of the traits that are typical of Attention deficit hyperactivity disorder (ADHD). In some cases it might be that these traits are disorderly only because of the ways in which current classrooms make demands on the attention of the pupils who are educated in them.[67] When they occur in certain other environments, hyperactive traits might not be disorderly in themselves. They might, in some contexts, be advantageous. A diligently attentive person might sometimes be unable to take advantage of opportunities that the fleetingly impulsive person seizes. Again the two sorts of contribution are likely to become entangled, if those social contexts that make hyperactive traits disorderly also contribute to the occurrence of such traits. That will be the case if, for example, one tends to be more distractible in those contexts where distractibility is an impediment.

For those who suffer from these conditions, social factors might contribute to the disorderliness of life, both by contributing to the bringing about of their symptoms, and by making those symptoms into disorderly ones. Had the social context been different, the symptoms might have been different. And, even if the symptoms had been the same, they might not have been so disorderly in a different social context.

Having drawn these distinctions between different social contributors to mental disorder, an ethical question comes into view. The following chapter considers it.

# Notes to Chapter 2.1

The illustration on Part Two's first page is based on a 1967 photo, "The Ultimate Confrontation: The Flower and the Bayonet," by Marc Riboud. (© Marc Riboud/Magnum Photos.) The image is used here with the permission of Magnum Photos.

55    The notion of human flourishing that we are using here is, as we have noted, an ancient one, but the idea that this notion should play a central role in our thinking about ethics (instead of giving that role to such notions as rights, or goods, or duties) was somewhat marginalized until the second half of the twentieth century, when the philosophical movement known as Virtue Ethics underwent a revival.  Rosalind Hursthouse's 1999 book *On Virtue Ethics* (Oxford University Press) provides a thorough introduction to the topic.  Philippa Foot's 2001 *Natural Goodness* (Oxford University Press) uses the notion of flourishing as the basis for her attempt to show how a place can be found for moral facts within the natural order.

56    The idea that families can be a source of mental disorder clearly has much to recommend it, from the point of view of common sense.  Evidence that this idea is indeed correct can be found in L. Rena Repetti, Shelley E. Taylor, and Teresa E. Seeman, "Risky families: Family social environments and the mental and physical health of offspring." *Psychological Bulletin* 128, no. 2 (2002): 330–366. This plausible idea should nonetheless be handled with care, since it can too easily turn into the unhelpful suggestion that, for example, mothers are always to blame for their children's problems.

57    It should be no surprise that one's partner can influence one's mental well-being.  The data supporting this are clearest (because easiest to gather) if we consider marriages.  Rates of marriage and divorce correlate with all sorts of health outcomes, both mental and physical.  Yuanreng Hu and Noreen Goldman make an international survey of these correlations in their 1995 review article "Mortality differentials by marital status: An international comparison." *Demography*, 32, no. 4 (1995): 483–507.  The more specifically psychological health outcomes of marriage and divorce are examined by Robin W. Simon in his paper "Revisiting the relationships among gender, marital status, and mental health." *American Journal of Sociology* 107, no. 4 (2002): 1065–1096.

Research into other sorts of sexual relationship is harder to conduct – and it is especially difficult to establish clear evidence of causation, rather than mere correlation – but here too the research that has been done supports the very plausible idea that one's relationship to one's partner can interact strongly with one's mental health.  Galena K. Rhoades, Claire M. Kamp Dush, David C. Atkins, Scott M. Stanley, and Howard J. Markman discuss the psychological impact of the ending of relationships other than marriage in their 2011 paper, "Breaking up is hard to do: The impact of unmarried relationship dissolution on mental health and life satisfaction." *Journal of Family Psychology* 25, no. 3 (2011): 366–374.  In a paper from the same year, Jesse Owen and Frank D. Fincham discuss the psychological effects of sexual relationships that do not involve romantic attachment: "Effects of gender and psychosocial factors on 'friends with benefits' relationships among young adults." *Archives of Sexual Behavior* 40, no. 2 (2011): 311–320.

58    "Social peers" come in many forms, and sociologists have a lot to say about many of them.  One form of peer relationship that seems to be particularly relevant to one's mental well-being is the having of a best friend in childhood: Catherine L. Bagwell, Andrew F. Newcomb, and William M. Bukowski discuss the evidence for this in "Preadolescent friendship and peer rejection as predictors of adult adjustment." *Child Development* 69, no. 1 (1998): 140–153.

59    The role of broad social factors in determining the well-being of particular individuals has been a topic of dispute in sociology, ever since that discipline first became established.  Émile Durkheim's 1897 book *Le suicide* (*On Suicide* (Free Press)) found that rates of suicide were consistently higher among Protestants than Catholics, and higher in both of these groups than they were among Jews.

Durkheim suggested that – although such factors are unlikely to be in anyone's mind at the time when they end their life – the relative suicide rates in these populations might be explained by reference to broad social factors, relating to the ways in which individual and social control are conceptualized differently in these three cultures.  This work played an important role in the establishment of sociology as a discipline.

Questions about the explanatory force of such social facts, as distinct from facts about individual psychology, have a foundational role in the philosophy of the social sciences.  Steven Lukes provides a still-useful discussion of some of the ideas that can be found in this part of philosophy in his 1968 article "Methodological individualism reconsidered." *British Journal of Sociology* 19, no. 2 (1968):119–129.

60    The literature on eating disorders is large, and a diverse group of risk factors has been identified within it.  For a discussion of the ways in which individual peer relationships can operate as risk factors for the Eating disorders, see Melissa Lieberman, Lise Gauvin, William M. Bukowski, and Donna R. White's

2001 paper "Interpersonal influence and disordered eating behaviors in adolescent girls: The role of peer modeling, social reinforcement, and body-related teasing." *Eating Behaviors* 2, no. 3 (2001): 215–236. For a discussion of the way in which family relationships can contribute to disordered eating, see Heather Patrick and Theresa A. Nicklas, "A review of family and social determinants of children's eating patterns and diet quality." *Journal of the American College of Nutrition* 24, no. 2 (2005): 83–92.

61    J. David Hawkins, Richard F. Catalano, and Janet Y. Miller give a thorough review of the factors that can increase the risk of developing a Substance use disorder in their paper: "Risk and protective factors for alcohol and other drug problems in adolescence and early adulthood: Implications for substance abuse prevention." *Psychological Bulletin* 112, no. 1 (1992): 64–105. Their paper is especially clear in its marking of the distinction between those factors that involve social norms, and those that involve what these authors call "individual and interpersonal factors."

The role of individual peer relationships in substance use is the particular focus of David M. Fergusson, Nicola R. Swain-Campbell and L. John Horwood, in their paper, "Deviant peer affiliations, crime and substance use: A fixed effects regression analysis." *Journal of Abnormal Child Psychology* 30, no. 4 (2002): 419–430.

62    Psychiatry's need to synthesize ideas that have been developed across a range of academic disciplines – including some disciplines that see themselves as rivals – is often expressed as a commitment to adopting a "biopsychosocial model." This "model," which is an aspiration to include every level of enquiry, from the molecular to the social, is given its canonical formulation in George L. Engel's 1980 paper, "The clinical application of the biopsychosocial model." *American Journal of Psychiatry* 137, no. 5 (1980): 535–544.

63    The distinction that we draw here, between different ways in which social factors can contribute to mental disorder, is by no means the only distinction that might usefully be drawn when considering the interaction between society and health. Bruce G. Link and Jo Phelan consider a range of evidence, concerning the ways in which social factors can contribute to both mental and bodily disorder, focussing on stress as a mediating factor between changes in social circumstance and changes in health. They survey a range of thinking on these topics in "Social conditions as fundamental causes of disease." *Journal of Health and Social Behavior* 35, Extra Issue (1995): 80–94.

64    Christine A. Conelea and Douglas W. Woods provide a comprehensive review of the evidence concerning the influence on tics of social and emo-

tional circumstances in their paper "The influence of contextual factors on tic expression in Tourette's syndrome: A review." *Journal of Psychosomatic Research* 65, no. 5 (2008): 487–496.

65    Autism spectrum disorder affects people in a number of ways, some of which can be advantageous.  Consequences of this for the way in which we should think of the condition are discussed by Simon Baron-Cohen in his paper, "Is Asperger syndrome necessarily viewed as a disability?" *Focus on Autism and Other Developmental Disabilities* 17, no. 3 (2002): 186–191.

66    Michelle A. O'Riordan, Kate C. Plaisted, Jon Driver, and Simon Baron-Cohen give a demonstration of one context in which autistic traits are advantageous in their paper, "Superior visual search in autism." *Journal of Experimental Psychology: Human Perception and Performance* 27, no. 3 (2001): 719–730.

67    Discussions of social contributions to the disorderliness of Attention deficit hyperactivity disorder (ADHD) can be found in Eric Carbone's "Arranging the classroom with an eye (and ear) to students with ADHD," published in *Teaching Exceptional Children* 34, no. 2 (2001): 72–82, and also in Linda J. Graham's "From ABCs to ADHD: The role of schooling in the construction of behaviour disorder and production of disorderly objects," published in *International Journal of Inclusive Education* 12, no. 1 (2008): 7–33.

## 2.2 Are We Changing People When We Should Be Changing Societies?

We have said that, like facial birthmarks and unlike lung cancer, some mental disorders might lose their disorderliness (or might, at least, lose *some* of their disorderliness) if their social context were different. This suggests that orderliness could be restored, at least in part, by the making of a social change.[68]

Social changes that would be conducive to mental order can often be hard to imagine, but there are some cases in which it is clear enough what sorts of change would be needed: The symptoms of Autism spectrum disorder might be less disordering in a context where single-mindedness was esteemed more highly; the symptoms of Attention deficit hyperactivity disorder (ADHD) might be less detrimental to flourishing in a context where education proceeded through something other than classroom teaching; and the symptoms of Tourette's disorder might be somewhat less disordering if we could find a social context in which self-control was required less frequently (although there would continue to be some ways – discussed later in this book – in which Tourette's disorder might still be bothersome to those who suffer from it).

The social reforms that could bring about such changes would be hard to design, and even harder to implement, but that is no reason to think that their implementation would be anything other than a good idea. It certainly sounds like a good idea to reform society, so as to make it easier for the diverse individuals in that society to flourish. It sounds like a rather more sinister prospect to be changing individuals, so as to make their flourishing better conform with the requirements of the social context in which they find themselves.

Psychiatry can play a role in bringing about changes of both sorts. It can help families, schools, and workplaces to become places in which human flourishing is more easily achieved, and in which it is achievable by a more diverse group of people.[69] It can also help individual patients to make the changes that will bring flourishing within their reach, given the social context in which they currently find themselves.

Interventions of this second sort could be described as cases in which people are being changed, in order to bring them into compliance with the demands of a broader society. Describing psychiatric interventions in that way reveals some of the reasons why the practice of psychiatry raises moral issues that go beyond the usual realm of medical ethics.[70] But the sinister tone of this description may prove to be misplaced.[71] We need to think carefully about how it should be assessed.

Careful thinking about this issue has sometimes been impeded, in cases where the stakes are tragically high. The medical expertise of psychiatry endows it with power. Governments have on occasion arrogated this power, in order to use it for political ends. The results have been oppressive. An example was reported by *The Economist,* in January 2017:[72]

> Last year Li Tian (not her real name) spent a month in a mental hospital. She has suffered from depression for years, but was not particularly low or anxious at the time. It was just that world leaders were preparing to gather in Hangzhou, the eastern city where she lives, for a G20 summit. Ms Li manages her illness with medication, but the authorities have it on record that she can be "unstable" (their evidence: she spent three months in a psychiatric hospital with postnatal depression some years ago). The government did not want any public outburst to mar what it saw as a hugely important event. So "someone from the community" visited her father, Ms Li says, and "suggested" that she check in to a psychiatric facility. Sufferers are still routinely treated as a danger to society.

It is not only when mental illness is treated as a political matter that there is a risk of psychiatry's authority being used oppressively. There is a similar risk when political dissent is treated as if it were a psychiatric matter.

Again there are examples from our current century – examples in which political dissidents have been treated as if they were mentally ill, have been incarcerated, and subjected to compulsory psychiatric treatment. In October 2014, after he had taken part in a protest prior to Vladimir Putin's inauguration for a third term as president of Russia, Mikhail Kosenko was sentenced to indefinite psychiatric treatment, having been convicted of rioting, and of assaulting a police officer. As *The Guardian* reported:[73]

> Despite witness testimony and publicly available video footage showing that Kosenko had tried to move away from a nearby scuffle during which a riot police officer was struck, a judge found him guilty and sentenced him to indefinite compulsory psychiatric treatment, concluding that his mental condition made him a danger to society. The riot policeman whom Kosenko allegedly struck told the court he did not know the defendant and could not remember who had struck him.

> Kosenko has mental health issues after a concussion during an army hazing incident nearly two decades ago but has undergone outpatient treatment.

Such cases illustrate the two main ways in which the rhetoric of psychiatry can be politically misappropriated: mental disorders can be misidentified as political threats, and political threats can be misidentified as mental disorders. The existence of such cases should remind us that, when we are considering psychiatry, we are considering something that can be used in a manner that poses a threat to our rights.

We should nonetheless be wary of supposing that psychiatry as a whole is morally compromised by the fact that there have been such cases. The authority of medicine quite generally has been abused in all sorts of historical contexts, and for all sorts of purposes, some of which are relatively trivial (as when the trappings of medicine are used to promote cosmetics), and some of which are much graver (as when the language of preventative medicine is used to promote eugenics). Medical rhetoric's proneness to this abuse makes it incumbent on doctors to be cautious. It would be an overreaction to take it as discrediting the whole of medicine. We should be similarly wary of calumniating all of psychiatry, merely because oppressions have sometimes been perpetrated under the guise of psychiatric treatment. The risk of having one's rhetoric appropriated is a risk to which every authority is vulnerable, however benign that authority might be.

This is not to say that psychiatry has no moral case to answer, only that the case needs to be considered judiciously.[74] In the 1960s and 1970s, the rejection of psychiatry became part of a wider anti-authoritarian counter-culture, at least in the industrialized West.[75] The case against psychiatric treatment was sometimes presented rather dogmatically. Psychiatrists were depicted as humorless administrators of tranquilizers, electroconvulsive therapy, and worse. Anti-psychiatric thinking became popular.

In some quarters the reputation of psychiatry has never entirely recovered. The stereotypes on which this reputation depends are, no doubt, unfair ones. If they are stereotypes that discourage the mentally ill from seeking professional help, and if they increase the stigma that is associated with receiving such help,[76] then they may also contribute to suffering. But again we should be judicious in making our assessment. Psychiatry cannot adequately answer the charges that have been brought against it merely by making the counter-accusation of stereotyping: all sorts of groups have been the subjects of unfair stereotyping, whether the activities of those groups were good, bad, or neither. Psychiatry can show itself to be innocent of the moral failings with which it has been charged, only to the extent that it addresses the issues by which these stereotypes have been motivated.

We can begin to approach those issues, somewhat obliquely, by returning to our earlier example of Tourette's disorder.

We said earlier that, rather like a facial birthmark, the symptoms of Tourette's disorder may be detrimental to a person's flourishing largely because of the social context in which those symptoms occur. When gauging the moral significance of this, we should remember that, although social context contributes to the disorderliness of these symptoms, it is not the only contributor. We can still recognize the symptoms of Tourette's disorder as being disorderly, even if we consider those symptoms from the patient's own perspective, without taking any account of the social norms with which they might conflict. The tics that characterize Tourette's disorder are controllable only temporarily, and only with effort. The experience of them is disorderly, not only because tics are socially deprecated, but also because they are moments in which control of oneself is lost. It is lost in a way that can, in some cases, impair the patient's capacity for executing complex actions. And − since our reasons for taking such a capacity to play a role in human flourishing do not depend on any arbitrary social conventions − it is not merely an arbitrary social norm that we are enforcing when we treat these tics as an impairment.

This verdict is not threatened by the fact that it might be possible to find a social context in which the Tourettic loss of control over one's movements was less debilitating. It might indeed be possible to find such a context, and it might be good to do so, but it would not be in anyone's interests to establish a society in which the loss of one's ability to perform unimpaired actions was normal, and was not understood to be disorderly. The case of Tourette's disorder is therefore one in which there are good reasons to seek a remedy that involves treatment of the patient, rather than seeking to undo the disorderliness of their symptoms only by changing our social norms.

A commitment to treating the patient does not mean that we are thereby ignoring the possibility that our social norms might also be changed. Changes to the patient and to society are both possible. Neither of these changes need be coercive. On the occasions when a psychiatrist is treating the patient, rather than agitating for a social change in which that patient's condition is regarded as normal, they need not be being oppressive. This particular case is therefore one in which the anti-psychiatric arguments that characterize treatment as an example of social coercion seem not to hit their target.

The case of Tourette's disorder is just one example, picked here for the sake of simplicity. By itself it does not suffice to address the more general moral question, especially since we have acknowledged that this particular disorder differs from others in a number of ways, and that it is, in some respects, an atypical case. As often in philosophy, we should enrich our diet of examples before reaching any general conclusion.

When we do consider a broader range of examples, and especially when we consider disorders in which the symptoms are more severe, the case for the non-arbitrariness of psychiatric treatment becomes clearer, but not unquestionably so. We can see some of these more severe cases by considering mental disorders that involve hallucination, delusion, or some other loss of contact with reality.

Again it might be possible to find a social context in which no disadvantage would be incurred by the people experiencing these symptoms. Perhaps there have been societies in which experiences of hallucination and delusion have seemed to be positively conducive to flourishing, on account of being regarded as qualifications for the high-status role of shaman.[77] Opponents of psychiatry have often drawn attention to the possibility of such societies, in order to expose the fact that there are alternatives to our own society's treatment of these conditions as disorderly. They have taken the existence of such societies to be an embarrassment for psychiatry, since the possibility of these societies shows there to be alternatives to the treatment of delusions as pathological, and thereby raises the question of why a pathologizing treatment is to be preferred to those alternatives.

It might seem to be obvious that no motivation for preferring our present approach could be derived from the interests of those people who we presently diagnose as suffering from delusional beliefs. Surely, one might think, these people would prefer to be treated as the venerable bearers of shamanic insight, rather than being told that their condition is a pathological one. But this seemingly obvious appearance should be questioned. Delusional beliefs often play a role in some larger scheme of paranoid or grandiose thinking, which may be distressing in itself, which may prevent the deluded person from forming normal relationships, and which may lead them to harm themselves or others. Although there may be social contexts in which the having of such beliefs would be venerated, it

is by no means obvious that those contexts would enable these several harms to be avoided. In order to help somebody to flourish, and to avoid suffering, it is not enough merely to venerate them.

In light of this, we can see that it may not be in anyone's interests – not even the interests of the deluded – to bring about a social change in which delusions are regarded as venerable, rather than disorderly. It may therefore be that the disorderliness of these conditions *is* best addressed by the treatment of the individual, rather than by the institution of a social change in which the conditions are no longer recognized as disorderly. As in the other cases that we have been considering, some combination of approaches seems likely to be best, with psychiatry working to treat the condition of delusional patients, while also working to find a social context that mitigates the detrimental effects of living with their condition. In our attempt to find such contexts, we might have a lot to learn from those societies in which delusional beliefs are a qualification for shamanic status,[78] but there is no reason to suppose that the lessons to be learnt here should lead us to abandon our current approaches.

The opponents of psychiatry might insist that this line of response addresses only a part of their complaint. They might insist that the real issue is a more fundamental one. Whether or not psychiatric treatment can further the interests of deluded people, by enabling them to avoid the distress, isolation, and harm that a delusional world-view might precipitate, these opponents of psychiatry might complain about psychiatry's entitlement to make a diagnosis of delusion in the first place. Such opponents would ask what it is that entitles the psychiatrist to take the having of paranoid or grandiose beliefs as grounds for the making of any sort of *diagnosis*. We do not, in general, think that people who have radically different beliefs from our own should therefore be thought of as having a diagnosable condition. Even the most thoroughgoing disagreements of belief are tolerated, in all but the most totalitarian societies. When these disagreements need to be addressed, they should be negotiated by the sharing of evidence and arguments. The parties to such a disagreement would find it hateful if their opponents first insisted on classifying their position as pathological. The challenge for psychiatry is to explain why its diagnosis of delusions is not at odds with this very basic recognition of the right to one's own beliefs about the world.

Psychiatry can begin to answer this part of the anti-psychiatrist's challenge by insisting that its diagnosis of delusions does not count people as ill merely on account of having a disagreement with the contents of those people's beliefs. The diagnosis of delusion implies a loss of one's capacity to bring one's beliefs into a state of properly responsive contact with the world, as one experiences it. The peculiar contents of one's beliefs might be evidence of this capacity having been lost, but the peculiarity of those belief-contents does not, by itself, suffice for the application of a psychiatric diagnosis. Restoring a person's capacity for bringing their beliefs into contact with the world does, of course, change the content of those beliefs, but psychiatry's reason for diagnosing delusions is not that it refuses to tolerate the possibility of people whose beliefs have different contents from our own.

The opponent of psychiatry might respond to this by reiterating their case. To do so would be to claim that psychiatry is still guilty of an unwarranted imposition, in its insistence that people should exercise a capacity to bring their beliefs into responsive contact with the world. If a deluded person does not care to regulate their beliefs in this way then, the opponent of psychiatry now contends, psychiatry has no right to insist that they should.

66

This reiterated challenge can be met with a reply that comes in two parts. The first part emphasizes the fact that the claim being asserted by the anti-psychiatrist is now a conditional one. Their claim is that *if the delusional person does not care to bring his beliefs into contact with the world*, then psychiatry has no right to treat his failure to do so as a diagnosable condition. Even if we were to grant it, this claim would be quite compatible with thinking that the diagnosis of delusion continues to be appropriate in all of those cases where people *do* care to bring their beliefs into contact with the world. The second part of our reply can then go on to say that all of the cases that a psychiatrist might actually encounter will be cases in which this condition is indeed satisfied. The people who receive psychiatric treatment do care about their beliefs being in contact with reality. And caring about this is not an arbitrary feature of our culture, which psychiatry coercively imposes upon them. Instead it is an immediate consequence of the fact that believing some claim just is taking it to be true of the world. To believe something is already to care about whether the world is as one believes it to be.

In making this reply, we have conceded that the justifications for psychiatric diagnoses make reference to values. The point to notice is that the justification can still be a good one, provided that the values are. In the diagnosis of delusion, the value that has a role to play is the value of truth. That is a value that should be acknowledged by anyone who has any beliefs at all. The anti-psychiatrist can avoid this conclusion only if they adopt a self-defeatingly sceptical position, by ceasing to care about truth, and so ceasing to have any beliefs.

Although they take us further than we could get by considering only the special case of Tourette's disorder, the foregoing lines of thought provide no more than a partial answer to our original worry. That worry arose because changing people so that they are better able to conform with the norms of our society sounded oppressive, whereas changing society so that diverse people are better able to flourish within it sounded like an unequivocally good idea. This had the consequence that psychiatry, insofar as it pursues changes of the first sort, could be made to seem rather sinister. We have been trying to determine whether that sinister appearance is justified.

We can continue to address the point by remembering that, here as elsewhere, what sounds like an unequivocally good idea may not be within the realm of the possible.

Social changes that would enable the simultaneous flourishing of all those suffering from psychiatric conditions would not be possible if the changes that would enable the flourishing of one group turned out to be incompatible with the changes that would enable the flourishing of another. It seems very likely that there would be such incompatibilities. The social changes that would best enable the flourishing of the person with Autism spectrum disorder are unlikely be compatible with the changes that would best enable the flourishing of the person with Histrionic personality disorder. The changes that would best enable the flourishing of the person with Hoarding disorder are unlikely to be compatible with the changes that would best enable the flourishing of the person with claustrophobia. It therefore seems likely that a psychiatrically *ideal* social change would be impossible. Any change that could actually be implemented would require compromises.

This should not be surprising. Here, as in every other political predicament, the interests of different groups will need to be balanced against one another.[79] Those whose interests are not being maximized under any particular arrangement may feel that they have been coerced. They may be justified in feeling this, but the only workable arrangements are likely to be ones in which *someone* feels coerced. Perhaps the optimal arrangement is a situation in which *everyone* feels coerced sometimes. Each particular accusation of coercion deserves to be taken seriously. But, since the good society may be one in which some small and broadly distributed amount of coercion is required, however regrettably, psychiatry need not be innocent of coercion in order to have a salutary role in that society.

To say that a psychiatrically ideal social change may not be possible is not to deny that there are some fundamental social changes that might usefully be made for the sake of mental health. We should remember that the possible extent and speed of social change has often been underestimated, especially by those who have a vested interest in the maintenance of the status quo. Our foregoing argument might be an example of just such an underestimation. It should not be taken as an argument in favor of complacency about the risks of psychiatric coercion. The psychiatrist should be careful.

But so should everyone else. It would be conducive to everyone's flourishing if our society were a kinder, more forgiving, and more sympathetic place. Insofar as the social contributors to mental disorder result from our various failures of moral imagination, it is incumbent on everyone to overcome those failures. This is not the job description of anyone in particular, and it is not a special burden to be carried solely by the psychiatric profession.

The issues that we have been exploring in this section can be understood as having started with an accusation. The accusation was that, whereas psychiatrists purport to be promoting health, just as other branches of medicine do, they are instead promoting a particular set of cultural values, these being the values that are embodied in one particular Western, individualistic, and capitalist conception of human flourishing.[80]

Disparaging things can be said about these values. They are values that have often been violently imposed on those with alternative conceptions of what human flourishing could look like. Their pursuit has damaged our environment, in ways that are quite possibly irreversible. It has entrenched all manner of social inequities.

Various attempts have been made to block accusations along these lines. Some of those attempts are, inevitably, more persuasive than others. One might attempt to face the accusations head-on, by disputing the disparaging things that have been said about Western capitalist values (although to do so would be to take sides in a much larger cultural debate). One might also reject the assumption that other branches of medicine operate with an objective and value-free conception of health. (To do that would not be to deny that there is a problem, but it would be to reject the idea that it is a special problem for psychiatry.)

The line of response that we have been considering in this chapter is different from both of these. It concedes the accusation's central claim – admitting that the conception of human flourishing promoted by psychiatry is indeed a value-laden one – but it denies that the practice of psychiatry is thereby shown to be imposing one particular and arbitrary set of values on those who would prefer to reject them. When considering the justification for diagnosing Tourette's disorder, we found psychiatry to be committed to a position in which the flourishing of humans is taken to involve their having a capacity to execute unimpeded actions. When considering the justification for diagnosing delusions as a symptom of a mental disorder, we found psychiatry to be committed to a position in which the flourishing of humans is taken to involve their having a capacity to form true beliefs. These *are* commitments of value, but they need not be arbitrary. They are often shared by the patients who are treated. The conception of human flourishing that they reflect plays a fundamental role in the social context within which flourishing needs to be achieved.

Not all disorders fit the model of Tourette's disorder, or of the disorders that are characterized by delusion, but these cases do illustrate the fact that the diagnosis of a patient need not be an arbitrary imposition upon them. We have also emphasized that the social changes required for a more equitable society are changes that psychiatry can help to bring about, not by oppressing those who suffer from mental disorder, but instead by contributing to the broader changes that would be conducive to their flourishing.

# Notes to Chapter 2.2

68    It is sometimes suggested that psychiatry ought to be primarily concerned with social changes, rather than with therapeutic interventions that center on the patient. This "community development" approach is said to be effective in those societies where it is normal. See, for example, Philip Thomas, Patrick Bracken, and Salma Yasmeen's paper, "Explanatory models for mental illness: Limitations and dangers in a global context." *Pakistan Journal of Neurological Sciences* 2, no. 3 (2007): 176–181.

69    Although we emphasize the difficulty in designing situations that are optimal for the mental well-being of all of the diverse people in them, some of the factors that have been found to correlate with psychological well-being are relatively simple ones. In a 2003 article – "The built environment and mental health," *Journal of Urban Health* 80, no. 4 (2003): 536–555 – Gary W. Evans reviews the evidence showing the impact on mental health of such environmental factors as noise, crowding, and air quality.

In the 1970s a number of people objected to the idea of psychiatry contributing to the reform of those social conditions that play a role in mental disorder, taking this to be a case of overreaching mission creep. Anthony Clare quotes Henry Miller:

> The Oxford Dictionary's definition of a psychiatrist is "one who treats mental disease." Not, you will observe, one who prevents wars, cures anti-semitism, offers to transform the normally abrasive relations between men into a tedium of stultifying harmony, is the ultimate authority on bringing up children or selecting directors, or misuses his jargon to confuse any and every topical issue in an incessant series of television appearances.
>
> (Miller, 1969, p. 44, quoted in Clare 1980 *Psychiatry in Dissent: Issues in Thought and Practice.* 2nd Edition London: Tavistock Publications, p. 63f.)

70    Any human practice, including any medical practice, can be studied from an anthopological point of view, and this point of view is one that rarely flatters. A classic example of cross-cultural anthropology being turned onto mental disorders, and the medical treatment of them, can be found in Roland Littlewood and Maurice Lipsedge's 1987 article "The butterfly and the serpent: Culture, psychopathology and biomedicine." *Culture, Medicine and Psychiatry* 11, no. 3 (1987): 289–335.

71     It is not generally considered sinister to remove a vascular birthmark, although this is our paradigm case of a condition that is disorderly only because of its social context. We should therefore distinguish between the question of where the disorderliness originates, and the question of where therapeutic interventions would best be directed.

72     "China wakes up to its mental health problems." *The Economist*, 28 January 2017.

73     Alec Luhn "Russian protester's sentence of indefinite psychiatric treatment upheld." *The Guardian*, 26 March 2014.

74     Andrew Scull gives a historically and geographically wide-ranging account of the ways in which psychiatric patients have been understood and treated in his 2015 book, *Madness in Civilization: A Cultural History of Insanity* (Princeton University Press). As Scull's book indicates, these treatments have too rarely been ones in which compassion and moral imagination play a central role.

75     At the height of the twentieth century's "culture wars," a key text for those who took all psychiatric interventions to be coercive was Thomas Szasz's 1961 book *The Myth of Mental Illness: Foundations of a Theory of Personal Conduct* (Harper & Row). R.D. Laing's 1967 book *The Politics of Experience and The Bird of Paradise* (Penguin Books) was also an influential contributor to this movement.

76     For evidence of the role of stigma in reducing access to appropriate treatment, see Georg Schomerus and Matthias C. Angermeyer's article, "Stigma and its impact on help-seeking for mental disorders: What do we know?" *Epidemiology and Psychiatric Sciences* 17, no. 1 (2008): 31–37.

77     The ancient Greeks took epilepsy to be a "sacred disease." The authoritative history of this was written by Owsei Temkin, in his 1945 book, *The Falling Sickness: A History of Epilepsy for the Greeks to the Beginnings of Modern Neurology* (Johns Hopkins University Press). For a review and discussion of the different cultural understandings of hallucination, see Ihsan Al-Issa, "The illusion of reality or the reality of illusion: Hallucinations and culture." *The British Journal of Psychiatry* 166, no. 3 (1995): 368–373.

78     The shaman depicted here is a Bedh Bahadur Gurung, who lives and works in the Northern Magar village of Taka, Nepal. He is shown with the drum that is used to summon his ancestral spirits, in a healing seance that is described by Piers Vitebsky in his remarkable 1995 book, *The Shaman: Voyages*

*of the Soul, Trance, Ecstasy and Healing From Siberia to the Amazon* (Duncan Baird). Vitebsky remarks on the tendency to over-simplify questions about shamanism and mental disorder when he writes:

> The shaman is a neurotic and a psychopath; the shaman is the sanest person in society, deeply sensitive to the moods of others; the shaman is a showman, conjuror and charlatan. All of these conflicting characteristics are regularly ascribed to shamans by observers, and all of them involve many assumptions about the shaman's personality and psychology. In view of the arduous nature of the shaman's calling, it is probably true that a distinctive personality is required, but the nature of this may vary. (p. 54)

The photograph of Bedh Bahadur Gurung on which our illustration is based was taken by Michael Oppitz in April 1978 (and it is reproduced in Vitebsky's book). Professor Oppitz reports that Bedh Bahadur is "the sanest and calmest person I have ever met in that professional calling. At the same time he is a great performer of ritual chants and regularly taken over by his helping spirits when working in a ceremony." We warmly thank Professor Oppitz (who owns the copyright) for his permission to use this image here.

79    The point here is, of course, a commonplace of social and political philosophy. No better discussion of it exists than that given by John Rawls in his 1971 *A Theory of Justice* (Harvard University Press).

80    The tradition of critiquing the Western Judeo-Christian capitalist value system is a long and varied one. The works of Friedrich Nietzsche (1844–1889) are a highlight of it. Nietzsche (who is portrayed on p. 69) suffered badly from mental disorder at the end of his life.

## 2.3 Sexuality and Disobedience

We have seen that some of the issues raised by psychiatry can rapidly lead us to foundational questions about social justice. Decisive answers to such questions can rarely be given. The responses that we have been considering to the anti-psychiatrist's accusations are not, of course, decisive ones. Nor do they apply equally in every case. The values that justify our treatment of delusions and of tics are unusual in being so plausibly fundamental. In cases where the values are more contested, the interplay between a person's condition and their social context will be more fraught.

In any particular case, those values will need to be considered on their own merits. The defense of psychiatric practice will then need to proceed in a piecemeal fashion, with different disorders – and perhaps even the individual cases of these different disorders – each being understood in different terms, depending on their contexts. One result of this is that different verdicts may be reached in different cases.

Cases involving the diagnosis of Oppositional defiant disorder raise a particularly problematic set of issues. The American Psychiatric Association's official criteria allow a diagnosis of Oppositional defiant disorder to be applied to those patients who display "a pattern of angry/irritable mood, argumentative/defiant behavior, or vindictiveness lasting at least 6 months." The criteria specify that this pattern of mood and behavior can include such things as loss of temper, being easily annoyed, arguing with authority figures, and refusing to comply with an authority's requests and rules. The diagnostic manual also notes, "It is not unusual for individuals with Oppositional defiant disorder to show the behavioral features of the disorder without problems of negative mood."

As criteria that are *sufficient* for a psychiatric diagnosis, these are problematic. Some authorities are oppressive. It is right to defy them. We may be justifiably angry about the need to do so.[81] Because the opposition of an authority may be justified, the angry rejection of authority need not be a psychiatric disorder, especially if this rejection happens "without problems of negative mood." Opposition to an oppressive authority may even be heroic. Something therefore seems to be amiss in the fact that, as stated, the American Psychiatric Association's criteria would allow that *any* angrily persistent defyer of an authority might be diagnosed with a psychiatric disorder.

Because they allow for diagnosis in too broad a range of cases, something seems to have been left unsaid by these criteria. We can easily see why it has been left unsaid: The thing that has been omitted is, broadly speaking, *political*. If we use the term "political" in a very broad sense, as we did above when quoting Aristotle's remarks about humans being political animals, then the question of whether some defiance of authority would be justified *must*, in part, be a political question: It must be a question about our relationships to the social structures that make a claim on us. The answers to such questions can never be made on the basis of wholly neutral considerations. Values must again play a role in the psychiatrist's decision to recognize that there is an instance of disorder. In this case – unlike in the earlier case of delusion, where the value at issue was the non-negotiably cardinal value of truth – it is in the nature of these political values that they might always be contested.[82]

Our opinion of any such diagnoses must therefore depend on what it is that we value. On the question of what we *should* value, the American Psychiatric Association quite rightly prefers not to offer an opinion. But this again forces it to dodge what can sometimes be an important issue, of a sort that psychiatric practice cannot help but raise.

The issues here are not only about political authority. Other fraught values that contribute to psychiatric diagnoses are those involving sex.[83] The second half of the twentieth century saw the emergence of a new understanding of the role that is played by sexuality in human well-being. Some of the distinctions that we have drawn above can help in providing an account of what it was that this new understanding achieved. They can also help us to see what might still remain to be done.[84]

The cases in which a disorder of sexuality would once have been diagnosed include cases in which a condition that was not disorderly in itself could nonetheless be detrimental to one's capacity for flourishing, on account of the fact this this condition occurred in a particular social context. In saying this we are not, of course, saying that being gay is or was like having a facial birthmark. But the cases do have something structurally in common: The social mechanisms that might make a facial birthmark unpleasant to live with were also once at work in making it unpleasant to live with homosexuality. [85]

As with other cases in which social mechanisms contribute to an impairment of flourishing, there was a possibility of attempting to treat the individual person, and there was also the possibility of a more cultural or political response, which changed the social context so that this person's condition was no longer an impairment to their flourishing. Prior to the moral progress in our understanding of sexuality, deviations from the heterosexual norm were assumed to be cases in which we did well to treat the person, instead of changing our society. A host of religious and political influences conspired to make it hard for people to imagine the social changes that would enable homosexuality to be compatible with human flourishing. The process of bringing about these changes is not yet complete.

Other sexual proclivities continue to be treated psychiatrically. When considering whether such treatment is appropriate, and how it might or might not be justified, there is a string of questions needing to be asked, each one of which can influence our answer to the others. We should ask, first of all, whether these proclivities are detrimental to anybody's flourishing. We can then ask whether the detrimental proclivities are *in themselves* detrimental to flourishing, or whether they are birthmark-like, in that they come to impair flourishing only because of their social contexts. If social contexts do contribute to the way in which these proclivities impair flourishing, we can go on to ask whether those contexts might be changed, so that flourishing was no longer impaired. And finally we can ask whether such social changes would be a good thing, all things considered. We should not expect any of these questions to be easy ones, nor any of the answers to be straightforward.

Asking such questions can nonetheless help us to identify reasons why some sexual proclivities *are* appropriate targets for psychiatric interventions, and it can help us to understand why some of them are not. The complexity of these issues can be seen by considering the example of voyeurism.

We can perhaps imagine a society in which a proclivity to voyeurism did not, in itself, diminish anyone's opportunities for human flourishing, below the level of flourishing that would be typical in that society. Perhaps there have been such societies in the past. These would need to have been societies in which the values of intimacy, privacy, and personal autonomy were understood in a way that was very different from our current understanding.

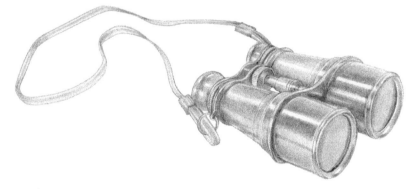

If we endorse the current understanding of these values, then we have good reasons to resist the social changes that would prevent voyeurism from being regarded as a diagnosable condition. The fact that Voyeuristic disorder continues to be diagnosable is an indication of our commitment to a particular conception of the ways in which intimacy, privacy, and autonomy are to be valued.[86] But – like the political values that contribute to the disorderly status of Oppositional defiant disorder, and unlike the alethic values that contribute to the disorderly status of delusions – the values that contribute to the disorderly status of voyeurism are not uncontested ones.[87]

Posters recently appeared in the city of Vancouver's buses, reminding men that it is illegal to share explicit photographs of their sexual partners without their consent. It is unnerving to learn that this fact needs to be advertised. The advertisement of it can be understood as one contribution to our public negotiation of these particular values – a negotiation that seems to have been necessitated by rapid changes to the ways in which we manage the flow of personal information. The consequences of this negotiation may not be so radical as to threaten our conception of the way in which voyeurism impedes flourishing, but something that is important to that conception does seem to be in contention.

The outcome of such value negotiations may need to be reflected in our psychiatric diagnoses, much as previous negotiations led the American Psychiatric Association to recognize such diagnoses as Female sexual interest/arousal disorder, or Male hypoactive sexual desire disorder.[88] All such negotiations involve something of value being at stake, and therefore being at risk. Things can be said for and against all such changes. Special care is needed when those who participate most prominently in these negotiations have an ulterior motive for doing so (as they might if, for example, they have a financial stake in a drug that can be used to treat some condition that is not currently recognized as being diagnosable).

Voyeuristic disorder is not the only case in which relevant values seem currently to be in contention. Instances of Transvestic disorder and Fetishistic disorder also raise some related issues. Transvestite and fetishistic proclivities might qualify, according to psychiatry's official diagnostic manual, as disorders, but – as with most other disorders – these can be diagnosed only if they cause "clinically significant distress or impairment in social, occupational, or other important areas of functioning." None of these predilections is counted as disorderly just by itself. Any of them *can* qualify as being disorderly, provided that this criterion of clinically significant distress is satisfied.

Since this last criterion plays a similarly central role in the great majority of our other psychiatric diagnoses, it seems to be this criterion that is doing most of the work in delineating the current limits of psychiatric diagnosis. Focussing on this general criterion of distress and impairment – and so focussing rather less on the particular criteria of each of the different diagnostic categories – might better reflect the role of those categories in actual psychiatric practice.

That practice is not only a therapeutic practice. It also includes pure research. We sometimes ask about the prevalence of mental disorder across a population, or about the long-term trends in the rate of occurrence of some particular disorder. For the purposes of addressing these population-level research questions, our diagnostic criteria tell us what it is that our statistics are counting. In these contexts the question of whether transvestism or sexual fetishes should be counted as disorders may be a rather abstract one. But in this regard the context of psychiatric research differs markedly from the context of therapeutic practice.

In therapeutic practice we are first of all confronted, not with an abstract question, but with a particular person who is in some state that causes them or those around them not to flourish. In such therapeutic contexts, our questions of diagnostic inclusion and exclusion are not questions of politics. They are, in many cases, questions of immediate practical importance. The diagnostic categories enable us to identify the existing patterns to which some particular instance of suffering conforms. A knowledge of these patterns can inform our attempts to alleviate that suffering. The enumeration of such patterns can therefore provide some orientation for our therapeutic efforts, without pretending to provide any general-purpose solutions, which are to be applied whenever some particular pattern is found. Psychiatry's diagnostic manual explicitly attempts to distance itself from any such general-purpose claims. Its role in therapeutic practice is never to specify a recipe by which mental health can be restored.

We might still need some objectively applicable criteria, for identifying and separating particular psychiatric conditions, or for the purposes of population-level research, but for therapeutic purposes we might hope to avoid a lot of nosological bother by letting the criteria of distress and impairment stand alone. Rather than needing to go through the more or less controversial process of specifying diagnostic criteria for Transvestic disorder, Sexual masochism disorder, and so on, we might instead try to say that any predilection that is harmful to oneself or others, to an extent that causes "clinically significant distress or impairment in social, occupational, or other important areas of functioning", will *ipso facto* count as being diagnosable. The details that would then be left out of our diagnostic categories need not be ignored. They could still be put into the clinician's notes.

This last suggestion raises an additional set of issues. Hitherto we have been thinking about the heterogenous set of mental disorders, and have been considering various matters arising when we ask what makes all of these conditions qualify as disorders, and what makes these particular disorders all qualify as being specifically *mental* ones. A new set of issues arises when, rather than considering the various mental disorders as a group, we instead ask about the classification schemes that divide this group into some particular set of diagnostic categories. These new issues pertain to the classifying of the disordered mind. Part Three of this book considers them.

# Notes to Chapter 2.3

81    The illustration on this chapter's first page is based on a 1956 photograph of Rosa Parks, seated at the front of a bus in Montgomery, Alabama. It is used here with the permission of Getty Images.

For recent discussions of anger's sometime appropriateness, see Amia Srinivasan's article "The aptness of anger" published in *The Journal of Political Philosophy* 26, no. 2 (2018): 123–144.

82    A commitment to the contestability of political values is itself a political value: one that is integral to liberal democracy, but that other ideologies might reject. This commitment is central to Karl Popper's political philosophy, as set out in his 1945 book, *The Open Society and Its Enemies* (Routledge).

83    It is sometimes suggested that more or less all of our thinking about the relation of sexuality to mental disorder is oppressive. That view can be found in Charles Moser's "Paraphilia: A critique of a confused concept", published in Peggy J. Kleinplatz (ed.) *New Directions in Sex Therapy: Innovations and Alternatives* (Taylor and Francis, 2001), 91–108. Its history is traced, with particular reference to the case of homosexuality, in Chapter Seven of Peter Conrad and Joseph W. Schneider's 1980 book, *Deviance and Medicalization: From Badness to Sickness* (C.V. Mosby).

A useful review of the literature on the diagnosis of sexual proclivities can be found in Alan G. Sobel's essay, "Desire: Paraphilia and distress in DSM-IV," published as Chapter Three of Jennifer Radden's 2004 *The Philosophy of Psychiatry: A Companion* (Oxford University Press), 54–63.

84    For an account of the history of this new understanding, see Gayle Davies' 2011 discussion, "Health and sexuality," published as Chapter 28 of Mark Jackson (ed.) *The Oxford Handbook of the History of Medicine* (Oxford University Press), 503–523.

85    The role of "stress associated with stigmatization based on sexual orientation rather than sexual orientation per se" is discussed by Michael R. Stevenson in his 2007 paper "Public policy, mental health, and lesbian, gay, bisexual and transgender clients", published as Chapter 16 of Kathleen J. Bieschke, Ruperto M. Perez, and Kurt A. DeBord (eds.) *Handbook of Counseling and Psychotherapy with Lesbian, Gay, Bisexual, and Transgender Clients* (Second Edition) (American Psychological Association), 379–397.

86    Our discussion of Voyeuristic disorder illustrates a point that arises as a consequence of our earlier claims about there being no biological or evolutionary criterion by which mental disorders can be distinguished from other atypical mental phenomena. In the absence of such criteria, we have seen (at the conclusion of Part One) that a broader conception of human flourishing must be used, when making assessments as to which conditions do, and which do not, warrant psychiatric intervention. We have said that this broader conception of flourishing includes social elements. Since the warrant for psychiatric interventions is therefore granted on partly social grounds, these interventions cannot be expected to enforce values that do not enjoy currency in the society within which our flourishing is achieved. And so psychiatry can operate morally only in a society with morally appropriate norms.

Voyeuristic disorder illustrates the risks that are associated with this. If voyeuristic behavior were to become socially normalized (which it might), then our social context would be one in which this would have ceased to be a diagnosable disorder. We cannot expect psychiatry to apply society-independent standards of "proper functioning," such as might save us from the harms that normalized voyeurism would bring with it.

The point that we are making here does not depend on any metaethical theory about the status of moral norms. It depends only on the idea that, whether or not the norms of morality itself are ultimately to be understood as being norms that should be relativized to particular social contexts, the norms that limit psychiatric intervention *are* so relativized.

87    Chrissy Thompson and Mark A. Wood give an account of the developments that have led us to a position in which the internet is routinely used for the non-consensual dissemination of intimate photographs in their article "A media archaeology of the creepshot." *Feminist Media Studies* 18, no. 4 (2018): 1–15. They also provide a clear account of the misogyny that these developments perpetrate, and reinforce.

88    In the particular cases that we mention here, there are some reasons to suspect that the cultural negotiations that have led to the recognition of these conditions are ones in which drug companies have played a profit-motivated role. Discussion of the cases in question can be found in Antonie Meixel, Elena Yanchar, and Adriane Fugh-Berman, "Hypoactive sexual desire disorder: Inventing a disease to sell low libido." *Journal of Medical Ethics* 41, no. 10 (2012): 859–862, and in Judy Z. Segal, "Sex, drugs, and rhetoric: The case of flibanserin for 'female sexual dysfunction.' " *Social Studies of Science* 48, no. 4 (2018): 459–482.

# Part Three: Dodging Nosology

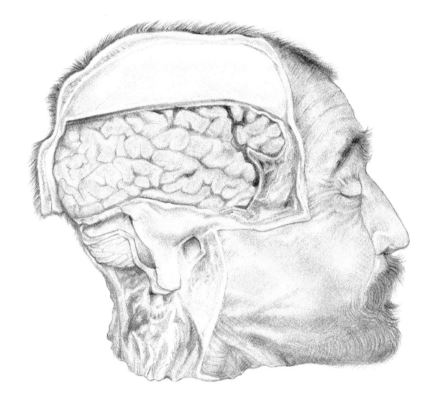

# Outline of Part Three

### 3.1 Psychiatric Diagnosis

Whereas receipt of a bodily diagnosis involves the acceptance of new information, receipt of a psychiatric diagnosis requires one to take a new perspective on one's own thought. That perspective is unlikely to be flattering, and may have some stigma associated with it. It is sometimes suggested that this assignment of patients to diagnostic categories is needless and unhelpful. A psychiatrist might therefore hope to avoid making diagnoses. Diagnostic categories might nonetheless be important for research, even if they are not crucial in therapeutic practice. They might also be socially important, in ways that are seen by considering the significance that attaches to the question of whether moderate cases of autism should be diagnosed as instances of a medical disorder. Recent debates about the status of psychiatry's diagnostic categories have been occasioned by revisions to its official diagnostic manual. It is sometimes suggested that these categories should be modeled on chemistry's periodic table of the elements. But disanalogies between chemistry and psychiatry make it unlikely that such unchanging categories could be defined.

### 3.2 Psychiatry Without Diagnostic Categories?

In addition to the idea that psychiatry might liberate itself from the need to assign patients to diagnostic categories, there is perennial appeal to the idea that mental disorders do not naturally divide themselves into such categories, since each person's experience of disorder reflects unique features of their character and situation. Although these ideas are undoubtedly attractive, they threaten to erect a barrier between the therapeutic practice of psychiatry and the scientific research that enquires into the basis of mental disorder. This chapter considers an argument that purports to show all scientific research to depend on the assignment of things to natural categories, with laws of nature that apply to them. It thereby reveals a tension between psychiatry's need to engage with the distinctive features of each individual patient, and its need to ground its therapeutic practice on the extrapolation of research findings from other patients, who fall into the same identifiable group.

### 3.3 Categories Unlike Chemistry's

A person's mental life is often apt to reflect the descriptions that she takes to apply to herself. Taking oneself to be cheerful, or taking oneself to be depressed, can therefore make a difference to the way in which one thinks and acts. Such attributions can sometimes become self-reinforcing. We see this mechanism at work not only in individuals, but also in groups, where it operates to give us such distinct and recognizable cultural identities as the goth, the hipster, and the beatnik. Such ways of categorizing people are somewhat unlike the systems of categorization with which science typically operates, but these categories are no less real on account of being unusual in this way. Although it is difficult to gauge how much of an influence it has, the mechanism of self-reinforcement also seems to play some role in explaining the ways in which mental disorders are experienced. There are several examples in which a culture's expectations of mental disorder seem to influence the ways in which mental disorderliness is experienced by the people in that culture.

## 3.4 Giving the Brain No More Than Its Due

Critics of psychiatry's current taxonomic scheme have recently suggested that a fresh start be made, building on new developments in our understanding of the brain, on developments in our ability to make observations of the metabolic activity taking place within a brain, and on developments in our ability to identify patterns in large bodies of data. This has tended to divert the attention of psychiatric researchers away from the social contexts within which mental disorder occurs, and towards the intrinsic features of the brains of those people who experience such disorders. It can seem hard to resist the idea that this is where the attention of these researchers properly belongs, since it is the brain that is most immediately responsible for the mental phenomena that are experienced as disorderly. It is, however, a mistake to expect the brain alone to provide explanations for disorder. Social context may still have an indispensable role to play, in enabling us to make sense of the explanatory import of the things that our observations of the brain reveal.

# 3.1 Psychiatric Diagnosis

There is a palpable load of emotion that accompanies the receiving of medical news, whether it is the news that some bone is or isn't broken, that some tumor is or isn't malignant, or even that some cough is or isn't the result of bronchitis, or of the common cold. In any course of medical treatment – whether psychiatric or not – the experience of being diagnosed can be a milestone, if not a turning point.

The evidence and inferences that go into making a diagnosis are often complex.[89] Our difficulty in digesting them can be made all the more severe by the accompanying emotions. And even when these emotions are relatively simple ones, people are often bad at weighing probabilities, partly because we are so bad at avoiding the influence of wishful thinking, and of the countless other biases that influence our thinking.

Knowing ourselves to be bad at avoiding bias, we are often willing to defer to the expertise of others, rather than digesting the complexity of diagnostic inferences for ourselves. When the diagnosis being made is a psychiatric one, this deference to the authority of experts incurs some complications.

When deferring to a psychiatrist, one must take this psychiatrist to have such expertise as is required for the making of a diagnosis, not only in general, but also in one's own particular case – a case that is always special, because one knows it so much more intimately than anyone else can, and knows it in so much more detail. This special intimacy that people have with their own minds adds a layer of complexity to the practice of psychiatric diagnosis, as compared to the diagnoses that are made in other areas of medicine. Even if you trust a surgeon and a psychiatrist equally, it may be easier for the surgeon to convince you that the pain you feel is not really a symptom of appendicitis than it would be for the psychiatrist to convince you the emotion you feel is not really the symptom of an anxiety disorder.

These complexities of psychiatric diagnosis vary from case to case. Psychiatric diagnoses are sometimes made on the basis of criteria concerning the unreasonableness of one's preoccupations, the unjustified status of one's doubts, or the disproportionateness of one's emotional responses: the person with Paranoid personality disorder is *unreasonably* fixated on persecution; the person with obsessive or delusional jealousy[90] is *unwarrantably* preoccupied with their partner's fidelity; the person with Adjustment disorder displays a level of distress that is *out of proportion* with the severity of its causes.

Whereas a bodily diagnosis merely provides one with information, the receipt of these psychiatric diagnoses requires a subtler change of mind. In accepting these diagnoses, we accept that someone else knows whether our doubts and fears are justified, reasonable, or proportionate. But that is not the stance of a person who is fully and sincerely gripped by those doubts and fears: were they sincerely gripped, the responses by which they are gripped would not seem disproportionate. Acceptance of the psychiatrist's authority to make these diagnoses therefore requires a peculiar stance towards one's own states of mind. Such cases are ones in which the process of psychiatric treatment cannot simply *begin* – as the process of medical treatment more typically can begin – with the supposition that diagnostic authority is granted. They are cases in which diagnosis needs special handling.

At the end of the second part of this book we saw a suggestion that seemed to enable many of the complications associated with such diagnoses to be avoided. The suggestion was that psychiatry could largely give up on the business of putting patients into diagnostic categories. The vocabulary that is currently used for diagnosis would still have a role to play in psychiatric practice, but its role would be merely descriptive, rather than classificatory. A course of psychiatric treatment would be occasioned merely by the recognition of a situation in which mental factors contribute to the impairment of some person's flourishing. The question of whether those factors belong to some recognizable category could be left open, perhaps indefinitely, without this being taken to imply that the culprit had yet to be unmasked, or that we had not yet reached the bottom of some mystery.[91]

In this book's third part we consider some of the reasons why this proposed demotion of our diagnostic categories is appealing, and some of the ways in which adopting this proposal would involve no real change to the way in which psychiatrists operate. We also consider some of the reasons why this idea might nonetheless prove to be a problematic one, on account of threatening psychiatry's conception of itself as an explanatory science.

Pursuing this agenda will require us to look at some of the different ways in which psychiatrists currently think about their diagnostic categories.[92] We conclude by considering the prospects for establishing a wholly new set of diagnostic categories, by applying the methods of artificial intelligence to the data that can now be gleaned from the scanning of normal and abnormally functioning brains.

### 3.1.1 Does Psychiatry Focus Excessively on Putting People into Boxes?

In his 1673 play, *Le malade imaginaire,* Molière satirized medicine's fondness for naming things.[93] One of the characters in Molière's play is a would-be doctor, who is asked by his examiners to explain the fact that opium sends people to sleep. The examiners are terrifically impressed when he replies that it does so because it possesses *virtu dormitiva.* This answer is greeted by them as a "*Bene, bene, bene, bene respondere.*" The joke is that the answer explains nothing at all. All that it means (in Latin) is that opium sends people to sleep because it has the power of sending people to sleep.

The explanatory emptiness of merely giving names to things is clear enough in the case that was imagined by Molière, and philosophers are forever indebted to him for providing this handy example, but there are cases from the real world in which it is less clear whether the application of a diagnostic label just gives us a redescription of the problem, framed in more official sounding language, or whether it also provides us with the beginnings of a real explanation. The reader will not be surprised to learn that some of these tricky cases are psychiatric.

We can imagine a parent being relieved to learn that their teenage child's recurrent habit of pulling at their own hair is a symptom of Trichotillomania, or that this child's angry outbursts are the symptoms of "Intermittent explosive disorder." Such acts of diagnosis would bring the child's difficult behavior within the doctor's remit. The child who was problematically angry could then be thought of as being angry in a way that is, at least, medically recognized.

That might be reassuring (and the value of reassurance should not be underestimated). It is nonetheless clear that a doctor's giving these names to things does not yet deliver any explanatory or therapeutic goods. These labels cannot, by themselves, explain very much: "Intermittent explosive disorder" is just another name for the distressing propensity to having disproportionate and explosive outbursts of anger. "Trichotillomania" is just another name (this one in Ancient Greek) for the recurrent hair pulling that causes apparent areas of baldness. It is easy to imagine what Molière would have thought.[94] Such terms might later be put to good use, but nothing explanatory is achieved merely by coining and applying them.

The charge from Molière is that diagnostic categorizations can sound like explanations, when all that they really achieve is a redescription. Since the act of redescribing someone's condition does them no obvious harm, Molière's charge is not an especially grave one. But it sometimes seems that something more serious is at stake. It is sometimes suggested that, by modeling its diagnostic practice on other branches of medicine, psychiatry prioritizes the assignment of people to categories *in ways that are not in the best interests of those people.* These critics suggest that assigning patients to psychiatric categories encourages us to think of their disorders as originating in the inherent dispositions of those patients, with the result that our diagnostic practices lead us to neglect any factors that exist outside of the patient, such as the social factors that we have seen can often play a role.

The charge here is not just that categorization fails to make things better, but that it actively makes them worse: In diagnosing Smith with an eating disorder, for example, we seem to imply that there is some problem that has its location *in the person of Smith.* Problems that have their location elsewhere, such as those that originate in unhealthy facts about Smith's society's dealings with food, with weight, with bodies, and with gender, are thereby relegated to the status of background conditions.[95] In making such a diagnosis, we might seem to imply that Smith herself is the primary location for a disorder that is better understood as being a failing on the part of her society.

This relegation of social factors to the diagnostic background may be unhelpful in lots of ways, but we may be able to avoid it without giving up on the business of diagnosis altogether. As our earlier discussion of facial birthmarks and Tourettic tics emphasized, it would be a mistake to suppose that social factors play no role in the explanation of disorderliness, even when a disorder does have an identifiable basis in the person who suffers from it. If there is a problem here, it originates, not in the project of psychiatric diagnosis, but in our habitual underestimation of background conditions. We can recognize those conditions as important causes of disorder, and as important targets for therapeutic intervention, whether or not we think of the disorders as belonging to distinct diagnostic categories.

It is sometimes thought to reflect badly on the priorities of psychiatry that the controversies surrounding the treatment of mental disorder are so often framed as controversies that concern the diagnostic categories with which psychiatrists operate.[96] The accusation here is that psychiatry directs its attention onto the business of categorizing patients, at the expense of considering the patients themselves.

That accusation might, to some extent, be based on a misleading appearance. Even if psychiatry's focus on diagnostic categories were entirely motivated by a concern for patients – so that its categories were evaluated purely for their usefulness in the daily business of helping people – those categories would continue to have a significance outside of such therapeutic practice.[97] Their broader ramifications might lend urgency to the controversies around psychiatry's diagnostic categories, while making the prominence of these categories larger than is warranted by their actual therapeutic use. The result of this would be that psychiatry's apparent preoccupation with diagnostic categories is not so bad as it might look from an outside perspective.

Stigma is one of these extra-therapeutic concerns, that can come to be associated with questions of psychiatric diagnosis. Regarding some condition as psychiatrically diagnosable tends to stigmatize the people who have it.[98] To the extent that it does so, there might seem *always* to be a reason for resisting the decision to regard a condition as diagnosable.

One example in which this reason seems to have some force is the case of Transvestic disorder, mentioned in the previous chapter. The cross-dresser who does not want to be treated as disorderly will not want their condition to be thought of as diagnosable. We should like to avoid stigmatizing them by insisting that it is, but we should also be careful not to follow this line of thought any further than it will go.

Because Transvestic disorder is diagnosable only when it causes "clinically significant distress or impairment in social, occupational, or other important areas of functioning," the cheerful and unencumbered cross-dresser does not have a diagnosable condition, according to our current diagnostic practices.[99] If we changed those practices simply by removing Transvestic disorder from the list of psychiatric diagnoses, this would entail that transvestism no longer gave any medical grounds for treatment, *even when distress is caused*. To rule that some condition is no longer diagnosable might remove the stigma from it. It would also imply that there can be no *medical* grounds for its alleviation.

In some cases this implication might be a welcome one (and transvestism may be a case in point). We have already noted that not every source of distress should be regarded as a disorder, even when that distress can be alleviated by psychiatric means. This was the lesson that we drew from our example of the not-quite-good-enough chess player. It is a corollary of this that we sometimes do well by freeing ourselves from medical obligations to alleviate suffering, if those obligations are, for example, patronizing ones. But it would surely be a mistake to think that we always do better by obliging ourselves to do less. When there are medical grounds on which special care is warranted, we should like to have diagnoses available with which those grounds can be specified, and with which particular conditions can be individuated, so that specific treatments for them can then be tested.

We should therefore be wary of any universally applicable arguments about whether psychiatry's use of diagnostic categories is, in general, a good or a bad thing. Our situation is always one of weighing reasons for and against, in each particular case. Even if stigma is, quite generally, a source of resistance, which the considerations in favor of diagnosis will need to overcome, considerations of suffering and disruption might weigh against these considerations of stigma with sufficient force that some condition should, on balance, be recognized as psychiatrically diagnosable.

The relative strength of considerations for and against the recognition of a diagnostic category is sometimes clear. In other cases it is not, with the result that it becomes contentious whether the case for diagnosis is strong enough to overcome the general reasons weighing against it. In any particular case there may be room for disagreement. The case of transvestism might be a relatively straightforward one. The case of Autism spectrum disorder is more than usually complicated, partly because this is a diagnosis that is often applied to children (to whom parents and governments have a special duty of care), and partly because the instances of it are so widely varied in their severity.

Those people with autism who do not want to be treated as sick will not want their condition to be thought of as a mental disorder, and will not want "Autism spectrum disorder" to be thought of as a diagnosis that applies in cases such as theirs. By recognizing Autism spectrum disorder as a diagnosis that applies even to mild instances of autism, we are able to understand our grounds for accommodating the special needs of a mildly autistic child as being *medical* grounds,[100] but the accommodation of such needs might also be thought of as being justified non-medically – and without any need for a potentially stigmatizing diagnosis to be applied. We routinely recognize the need to accomodate people who are left handed and people who are right handed, without needing to think of either condition as being a disorder that ought to be diagnosed. Our reasons for accommodating someone with mild autism might, similarly, be understood as being an acknowledgement of the diverse ways in which people think and learn, without the autistic condition or the non-autistic condition being thought of as a diagnosable disorder.[101]

The issues here are made complicated by the fact that there are different practical consequences, outside the context of therapy, of these different conceptions of the reasons why accommodations should be made. If the grounds for accommodating the special needs of a child with autism are medical ones then it is appropriate for the cost of those accommodations to be met from medical budgets. If we accommodate those needs as a part of our respect for the various ways in which different people learn and interact with their peers and teachers, then the cost of these accommodations falls within the range of what we would expect to be covered by the general budget for education.

The case of Autism spectrum disorder therefore illustrates one of the ways in which decisions as to the boundaries of psychiatric diagnoses can have consequences outside of the psychiatrist's therapeutic practice. The presence of such consequences will ensure that these boundaries are frequently debated, even if the therapeutic practice of psychiatry is not affected significantly by them. It is therefore understandable that the literature around psychiatry should be full of debates about diagnosis, even if the therapeutic business of psychiatry is one in which the making of a diagnosis is often uncontroversial. It might not matter, therapeutically, whether mild autism is thought of as a disorder, or as an instance of normal human diversity. It might nonetheless matter, politically, rather a lot.

Because of this, the energy that is devoted to debates around diagnostic criteria need not be a taken as a sign of any unjustified preoccupation on the part of psychiatry with the assignment of people to psychiatric categories. It might instead be taken as a consequence of the way in which psychiatric diagnoses interact with politics (broadly construed). Although psychiatry might inevitably provoke fractious debates concerning the limits of its diagnostic categories, this need not be because psychiatrists themselves care about the answers to those questions. If they do care, it is not necessarily because effective therapeutic practice requires them to.

It is nonetheless important that the diagnostic categories with which psychiatry operates should be the right ones, not only for external reasons of politics, and not only because words themselves matter – although sometimes they do matter rather a lot[102] – but also because the scientifically preliminary business of sorting things into nameable categories is itself important.

This impetus to categorize need not originate in any narrow-minded desire to pigeon-hole things. There are sound scientific reasons for wanting to put things into categories. These reasons operate across a range of medical and biological sciences. Faced with the great variety of, say, butterflies, it was a sensible first step for scientists to seek ways of grouping the individual butterflies into categories, and to look for particular features that make each category distinctive. Nobody would suggest that this project of categorization was ill-motivated, or that the pursuit of it revealed butterfly-lovers to be pigeon-holers, narrow-mindedly fixated on the assignment of things to categories. Once these categories had been established, it became possible to predict some aspects of the behavior of those individuals that had been classified correctly. The system of classification also provided a vocabulary in which lepidopterists could communicate efficiently.

Identifying the distinguishing features of each category may only be the first step in a larger explanatory project, but it is important that this step be taken, and that it be taken in the right direction. It is nonetheless true that, in the case of mental disorders – each instance of which depends on the idiosyncratic features of an individual sufferer's life and character – the motivation to classify is weaker than it is in the case of butterflies. Even if the desire for a classificatory scheme is well-motivated, there is less reason to suppose that our attempts at classification will be successful, or that they could ever be brought to a definitive conclusion.[103]

If the project of psychiatric classification could be completed successfully, it would bring all of the benefits that usually come with having an established taxonomic scheme: It might help us to predict the behavior and experiences of those individuals who have been classified correctly, and so might put us in a better position to help them. It might also provide a vocabulary in which therapists and researchers could communicate efficiently. But it is not at all obvious that this project is one that *can* be completed successfully. The process of defining and redefining psychiatric categories seems, instead, to be forever in contention.

*3.1.2 Why Does Psychiatry Struggle to Get its Classificatory Scheme in Order?*

Two lines of thought, both of which we have glimpsed, speak against the idea that a science of psychiatry should follow the example of the lepidopterists, by beginning with a taxonomy of psychiatric disorders. The first line of thought says that the categorization of psychiatric disorders gives doctors and patients an *unhelpful* way to think of mental disorder. The second says that the division of psychiatric disorders into categories is an *inaccurate* representation of them. Both lines of thought are contentious. Both should be handled with care.

These two lines of thought are distinct from each other, in the sense that one might take either line with or without taking the other. Just as it might be *useful*, if not accurate, for the zoo keeper sometimes to categorize the dolphins with the fish, so it might be *useful*, if not accurate, for the psychiatrist sometimes to classify an aversion to the sight of blood as if it were a phobia. Our diagnostic categories might, in general, be useful, even if they are not strictly speaking accurate.[104]

On the other hand, our diagnostic categories might not be useful – they might even be actively unhelpful – even if their accuracy is unimpeachable. Just as it might be unhelpful to think of oneself as an unpromising interview candidate, even in cases where that description is an accurate representation of one's chances, so it might be unhelpful to think of oneself as a person with an Anxiety disorder, even if that description would be accurate.

The question of whether it is therapeutically useful for a person to think of themselves as belonging in some psychiatric category is therefore distinct from the question of whether these diagnostic categories correspond to anything in reality. Despite this logical distinctness, our answers to the question of accuracy and the question of usefulness are, in practice, likely to interact. The controversies around psychiatric diagnosis have tended to be simultaneously concerned with both.

Those controversies have centered, in recent decades, on the *Diagnostic and Statistical Manual of Mental Disorders,* published by the American Psychiatric Association. This manual (from which we have quoted more than once, in the preceding discussion) is known to its advocates and to its detractors as the DSM. Its categorization of disorders has been revised on several occasions. And this ongoing process of revision has become a regular source of psychiatric contention.

The fact that the diagnostic categories of psychiatry have been subject to these rather frequent revisions is not, in itself, a sign that those categories are bad or arbitrary ones. We should expect there to be such revisions, as a part of any young science's development. It took chemistry a long time to realize that the halogen gases belong together in one group, and the noble gases belong together in another. It took an even longer time to understand why that should be so. These revisions to chemistry's scheme for the categorization of substances were a sign of progress toward the achievement of a satisfactory chemical theory. Earlier errors were corrected in the course of making these revisions, but the revisions themselves were not a sign of confusion or of arbitrariness.

In the relatively young science of psychiatry, some of the revisions that have been made to our classificatory schemes reflect changes in the theoretical approaches that have enjoyed most influence. These revisions have never avoided criticism, some of which has been aired publicly, and in forthright tones,[105] but, in a science that is still at an early stage of development, even these theoretically motivated revisions need not be a sign of confusion.

Few psychiatrists would expect this contentious process of taxonomic revision to converge on a single scheme in which all possible mental disorders are stably and exhaustively enumerated, in a way that provides uncontroversial criteria for their diagnosis. Even if such a convergence were possible and desirable, it would be unlikely to happen soon.

The ongoing need to revise our categorizations can therefore be taken as a sign of psychiatry's still-contested theoretical foundations.[106] But it can also be taken as a sign that psychiatry is a science in which no stable classificatory scheme could ever be had. The mainstream view in North American psychiatry seems recently to have been moving from the first of these interpretations to the second: whereas it previously tried to downplay the extent to which revisions to the DSM involved changes to the foundations on which it is built, the American Psychiatric Association now invites us to think about such changes as integral to the way in which psychiatry develops. The change in numbering, from the Roman DSM-IV to the Arabic DSM-5, was made in the expectation that some future editions of the book will be numbered DSM-5.1, and so on. It seems that this is intended to suggest that we think of changes to our psychiatric taxonomy in the same way that we think about the updates to the software that is running on our computers: The introduction of these changes is a process of constant adjustment and refinement, to which no end is yet envisaged.

One reason to prefer this second perspective is just that no science is ever *finished*. There are always more questions to be asked. The process of scientific discovery proceeds fitfully in its early stages. Even in its later stages, the goals of science are approached asymptotically. The scientific method brings us ever closer to the truth, without enabling us to know that some future discovery won't overthrow the theories that currently look to be well supported.[107]

A more psychiatry-specific reason for this taxonomic instability is that social contexts play a role in determining the ways in which mental disturbances manifest themselves, and those are contexts that are inevitably subject to change.[108] Because of that change, the process of redesigning our categorization scheme may never be complete, and may never be completable, not even in principle. If the goal of this process is constantly in motion, psychiatry's categorizations might need always to remain in contention.

### 3.1.3 Natural Kinds, and Other Categorizations

Rather than asking whether our current psychiatric diagnoses assign people to the most helpful or most accurate categories, we can also ask the more basic question of whether mental disorders should be divided into categories at all. This question is an important one, since we should be wary of supposing that distinct categories of mental disorder really exist.

It may be helpful here to consider an analogy between the study of the mind and the study of race and ethnicity. A central insight from turn-of-the-millennium thinking about race was that our grouping of people into races is something of an illusion, resulting from some general tendencies of human thought.[109] There is good evidence that humans are prone to thinking in categorical terms, even when a continuous and undifferentiated diversity characterizes the things that we are trying to understand. When these things that we are trying to understand are other people, this tendency can be pernicious.

If our attempts to understand people start from the supposition that those people fall into discrete groupings, each with its own distinct characteristics, then such groupings will seem to appear, as an illusion created by our propensity for thinking in stereotypes, together with our natural tendency to give too much attention to any evidence that confirms our views, and too little attention to any evidence that refutes them. It might once have seemed to be the case that people belong to distinct racial categories, each with its own distinguishing characteristics. We now know that the underlying reality is more complicated.

This phenomenon might be analogous to something that happens when we try to understand mental illness. It might be that psychiatric patients seem to exhibit distinct categories of mental disorder, when here too the reality is more complex and undifferentiated.

One preliminary piece of evidence against the existence of categorical distinctions is that there are often multiple diagnoses that some individual patient might receive. A patient who is diagnosed with Generalized anxiety disorder might also have been diagnosed as having a Persistent depressive disorder (dysthymia). Had they been diagnosed at a different stage in the course of their disorder, they might also have been diagnosed with, for example, Separation anxiety disorder. It is quite common for patients to present with overall complaints to which several diagnoses apply. This makes the assignment of patients to categories look like a rather more fragile business than the assignment of butterflies to their species, or the assignment of chemicals to their groups in the periodic table. In these other branches of science the assignments of things to categories are stable, and they typically display a kind of exclusivity: at any given level of the taxonomic hierarchy, there is just one category to which any given specimen belongs. Psychiatry's categorizations do not currently have either of these properties.

This is some reason to think that the groupings that we observe among mental disorders might be an imposition, resulting from our propensity to see things as falling into predictable categories, but it is certainly not a decisive reason. This question cannot be settled by our analogy with the notion of race, nor by the existence of any other mere analogy. Such analogies can only ever be suggestive. Knowing that humans have a tendency to stereotyping should make us cautious, but it need not make us give up on our taxonomic projects altogether. Science is full of examples in which, by carefully working to overcome our tendencies to mishandle evidence, we have arrived at classifications that are not arbitrarily imposed on the phenomena that we are trying to understand. Here, as elsewhere, the point can only be that we should work carefully. It is a reminder that we *might* have to give up on the search for discrete categories, not an exhortation for the search to already be given up.

Outside of psychiatry, in some of the longer-established branches of science and medicine, we can sometimes know that our groupings are not arbitrarily imposed because we can know that those groupings correspond to categories that already existed, prior to our attempts at scientific understanding. In the hope of finding such independently existing categories, psychiatrists have often taken these more established branches of science as a model. The most ambitious model to follow is that of chemistry.

The formulation of chemistry's periodic table took centuries.[110] Its eventual completion fixed our scheme for the categorization of chemical phenomena, and thereby provided the foundations on which a vast structure of scientific explanation could be built. Many psychiatrists aspire to a classificatory scheme in which the categories of mental disorder have the same foundational status. Our philosophical understanding of the categories that enjoy such a status owes a great deal to the work of John Locke.[111]

Locke was born in 1632,[112] and therefore lived at the time when alchemy was being replaced by what we now recognize as chemistry. The book in which the distinction of chemistry from alchemy became clear was *The Sceptical Chymist,* which was published in 1661. Its author – Robert Boyle[113] – was one of Locke's friends, and one of his intellectual allies.

The development from alchemy to chemistry changed our scientific understanding of the ways in which substances do and do not interact. That change brought with it a change in our conception of the way in which such scientific understandings are achieved. Locke wanted to account for the possibility of those achievements. As a part of his attempt to do so, he was interested in the classifications that chemists are employing when they apply a term like "gold."

Were we to have asked Locke, Boyle, and their contemporaries what gold *is,* they could, of course, have told us that it is a heavy, soft, yellow metal. They could also have told us about some further properties of it: ones that are more exotic than its heaviness, softness, and yellowness, and that can be observed more reliably and precisely when various laboratory tests are applied. These would have included such properties as ductility, being soluble in mercury, and being only weakly susceptible to the influence of magnetism.

It seems possible, on the face of it, for there to be something that has all of those properties – both the exotic and the quotidian – but yet is a mere doppelgänger of gold. Since it is conceivable that there might be such a substance, this was something of which early chemistry needed to be wary. Locke realized this, and so knew that the catalog of gold's observable properties could not be the whole story when it came to saying what gold *is*. To be real gold, it is not enough to duplicate these more or less superficial properties. To be real gold, and not a mere doppelgänger, a thing has to be made from the right kind of stuff.

Because the science of chemistry was still in its infancy, Locke was not in a position to know what it took for a putative sample of gold to *be* the right kind of stuff. He nonetheless realized that, whatever it was, this real essence of gold had to be distinguished from the profile of properties that show up in the lab, and that we use to test whether the name "gold" has been rightly applied. The properties that show up in the lab might give us a signature by which gold can be recognized, but they cannot be the real essence of the stuff. He called this more or less superficial profile of properties the "nominal essence" of gold, and distinguished between this nominal essence and gold's "real essence." At the time when Locke drew this distinction the properties that give the *real* essence of gold – those that make an instance of gold the stuff that it is – had yet to be discovered.

Centuries of chemical research successfully revealed the thing that Locke was not yet in a position to know. We can now say that the real essence of gold is identified by its place in a periodic table of the elements (at atomic number 79). Developments in physics over the course of the twentieth century enabled us to explain why stuff that is made from atoms with 79 protons in their nuclei should be a metal, and why it should have the properties of yellowness, heaviness, ductility, solubility in mercury, resistance to magnetism, etc.

Those explanations are a triumph of the scientific method. Sciences that have not yet attained the maturity of physical chemistry quite naturally take these explanations as a model. It should therefore be no surprise that some theorists of psychiatry aspire to a taxonomy of psychiatric conditions that has the established status now enjoyed by chemistry's periodic table.[114]

To take the periodic table as a model for psychiatric diagnoses would be to suppose that our current position with regard to the mental disorders is similar to Locke's position with regard to gold and the other elements. We can produce a list of properties for most of the disorders that psychiatry treats, with some of these properties being immediately manifest, and some of them being properties that show up in the lab, or when various tests are applied. Having this list of properties enables us to recognize instances of these mental disorders when we see them.

But, like Locke with gold, we do not yet have a picture telling us about the real underlying essences of these disorders, by which their several more or less superficial properties are to be explained. The criteria listed in the DSM-5 enable us to diagnose an instance of, for example, Autism spectrum disorder; but – perhaps because the science of biological psychiatry is as young for us as the science of chemistry was for Locke – we are only just beginning to have an account of there being an underlying real essence, by which the observable symptoms of the autistic condition are to be explained.

Since chemistry developed into such an extraordinarily precise branch of science, this Lockean analogy gives an attractive picture of psychiatry's classificatory ambitions. We should nonetheless be cautious. There is more than one way in which the analogy with chemistry might be misleading.

Gold was always out there, as the element whose atoms contained a total of 79 protons. It was there before we knew anything about atomic numbers, before we had realized that it must be an element, and before we had worked out what the chemical elements are. The progress of chemistry revealed the pre-existing facts about gold, but did not change those facts.

The mental disorders are not like that. Those disorders are not indifferent to us, or to our attempts at classification.[115] Whereas gold did not care what we thought of it, the people who we classify as having particular mental disorders very often do care.

Their behavior and thinking can be affected by their own understanding of the diagnoses that they are given, much as anyone can be affected by an awareness that they are an example of some particular human category, with which particular characteristics are associated.

Nor is there the same motivation for distinguishing between the real and nominal essences of psychiatric disorders. Whereas something might conceivably look and feel like gold while being a mere doppelgänger of it – and whereas something might look superficially like a butterfly while instead being a moth, or a subtly crafted automaton – somebody who has the full subjective experience of anxiety *is* therefore anxious: It would be absurd to try to convince them otherwise. Some disorders may have an as-yet-unknown real essence, by which their symptoms are to be explained, but there is no general reason to think that all psychiatric disorders must have such an essence, and there is no general reason why medical practice should want to rule out doppelgängers, as not being the real thing. If the replication of properties is sufficiently complete, and includes the having of the requisite first-person experience of the disorder, then – in the psychiatric case – a doppelgänger is the real thing.

The psychiatrist who hopes that psychiatry will follow the example of chemistry may therefore be hoping for something that is not needed, and that cannot be had. Whereas the properties that make up the nominal essence of gold have been explained as consequences of its unchanging real essence, the instances of Generalized anxiety disorder might not have any such common explanatory essence, lying behind the profile of properties and experiences by which Generalized anxiety disorder is identified. Rather than being a more or less superficial "nominal essence," this profile of manifest properties might itself be the heart of the matter. Those properties certainly are at the heart of the pragmatic considerations with which psychiatric medicine is fundamentally concerned.

This raises the question of how far our retreat from the example of chemistry should go. The therapeutic parts of psychiatric medicine are concerned with the genetic, biological, and neurochemical substrates of mental disorders only insofar as these enable us to understand and alleviate the distress and disorder that manifest themselves in the felt experience of people's lives. This has led some theorists to go so far as to claim that psychiatric diagnoses should be understood as a *purely* pragmatic matter, so that the assignment of patients to diagnostic categories is to be evaluated only for its therapeutic value, and not at all for its role in any broader scientific project of identifying the underlying structures and causes of their conditions. Other theorists worry that this holds psychiatry's classificatory scheme to too low a standard, since all sorts of spurious classificatory schemes might have a merely pragmatic value, as heuristic tools for making predictions about behavior, without those schemes being appropriate for the research that gives psychiatric interventions their evidential basis.

In light of the differences between chemical elements and psychiatric diagnoses, we may want to resist the idea that our position with respect to mental disorders is like Locke's position with regard to the elements. It does not follow from this that we should give up on the aspiration to have a systematic categorization of mental disorders, such as might enable us to get a clearer sense of which questions need to be answered in order for instances of mental disorder to be explained.[116] That would be a further claim, but it is a claim that has sometimes been advocated, both within the science of psychiatry, and by critics outside of it. We consider it in the next chapter.[117]

# Notes to Chapter 3.1

The illustration on Part Three's first page is based on an 1890 photograph. The photographer is unknown.

89    The complexities of diagnostic inference, and the difficulties of dealing with them, were brought to the attention of clinical psychologists in a now-classic paper from 1955, written by Paul E. Meehl and Albert Rosen: "Antecedent probability and the efficiency of psychometric signs, patterns, or cutting scores." *Psychological Bulletin* 52, no. 3 (1955): 194–216.

90    The illustration shows Maurice Brown as Iago and Paul Robeson as Othello, in a 1930 production at the Savoy Theatre, London. It is based on a photograph from p. 127 of Michael A. Morrison's article, "Paul Robeson's Othello at the Savoy Theatre 1930" published in *New Theatre Quarterly* 27, no. 2 (2011): 114–140, and is used here with the permission of Cambridge University Press.

91    It is not only in psychiatry that one might be attracted to the idea of medical interventions that work towards the promotion of health without needing to start by attributing one's current lack of health to some generalizable diagnostic category. Marc Lange makes the case for this broader claim, drawing on considerations from psychiatry and from other branches of medicine, in his paper "The end of diseases." *Philosophical Topics* 35, no. 1/2 (2007): 265–292.

92    Different conceptions of the classificatory schemes of psychiatry are discussed by Kenneth S. Kendler, Peter Zachar, and Carl Craver in their paper "What kinds of things are psychiatric disorders?" *Psychological Medicine* 41, no. 6 (2011): 1143–1150, and by Kendler alone in his "The nature of psychiatric disorders." *World Psychiatry* 15, no. 1 (2016): 5–12. A survey of the issues that are at stake in current debates about the basis of psychiatric diagnoses can be found in Şerife Tekin's "Psychiatric taxonomy: At the crossroads of science and ethics." *Journal of Medical Ethics* 40, no. 8 (2014): 513–514.

93    Molière's satire was not only directed onto the medical profession's fondness for giving names to things. He satirized many other features of medicine too, here and in his other writings.

94    The Molière-inspired charge against certain psychiatric diagnoses (in particular, against the Personality disorders) is made by Peter Zachar, in the entry on "Personality disorder: Philosophical problems" in Thomas Schramme and

Steven Edwards (eds.) (2017) *Handbook of the Philosophy of Medicine* (Springer), 1005–1024.

95     For the complaint that the category of Anorexia nervosa pathologizes the individual, when a broader social perspective would be preferable, see Derek Botha's article "Anorexia nervosa: A fresh perspective." *Theory & Psychology* 25, no. 3 (2015): 328–345. Similar considerations were developed by Colin Samson in "The fracturing of medical dominance in British psychiatry?" *Sociology of Health & Illness* 17, no. 2 (1995): 245–268. An older version of this complaint can be found, in a less academic context, in a 1976 article by Frances Seton, discussing her own experiences of psychotherapy: "Opening myself to change" reprinted in Marsha Rowe (ed.) *Spare Rib Reader* (Penguin Books, 1982), 410–416. Seton writes:

> I read all I could about psychology, which only provided me with a series of labels to describe my state and, more seriously, literally to hide behind. (A criticism I have of psychology and indeed medicine is that is gives problems a concrete existence separate from their origins.) (p. 413).

96     In "Culture, cultural factors and psychiatric diagnosis: Review and projections." *World Psychiatry* 8, no. 3 (2009): 131–139, Renato D. Alarcón remarks, "Diagnosis is probably the dominant topic of discussion and debate in the psychiatric field today" (p. 131). If that is true, it is not a new phenomenon. Already in 1938, Jules Masserman and Hugh Carmichael were writing, in "Diagnosis and prognosis in psychiatry: With a follow-up study of the results of short-term general hospital therapy of psychiatric cases." *Journal of Mental Science* 84, no. 353 (1938): 893–946:

> The prognostic and heuristic value of the present system of psychiatric nosology of the neuroses and minor forms of the psychoses is challenged by the high incidence of "mixed" cases in our series, and by the fact that during only a year of follow-up study a major revision of the "diagnosis" had to be made in more than 40% of the patients. (p. 931).

97     Anthony Clare gives an accessible account of psychiatric diagnoses, although it is by now a somewhat dated one, in Chapter Three of his 1980 book, *Psychiatry in Dissent: Controversial Issues in Thought and Practice* (Tavistock Publications).

98     The stigma associated with psychiatric diagnoses was much emphasized in the "labelling theory", discussed by Thomas J. Scheff in his 1974 article, "The labelling theory of mental illness." *American Sociological Review* 39, no. 30 (1974): 444–452. The "labelling theory" also anticipates some of the

ideas about "looping effects" and self-stereotyping, which we discuss later in this book.

99    The cross-dresser depicted here is the late Paul "Laverne" Cummings, one of San Francisco's trailblazing female impersonators. Our illustration is based on an image in the personal collection of David De Alba, and is used here with his kind permission.

100    The large body of research into Autism spectrum disorder includes a considerable amount of work looking at the way in which autistic thinking can be supported in educational settings. An authoritative review can be found in the 2014 *Handbook of Autism and Pervasive Developmental Disorders (Vol 2.) Assessment, Interventions, and Policy* (John Wiley & Sons), edited by Fred R. Volkmar, Sally J. Rogers, Rhea Paul, and Kevin A. Pelphrey, especially in the chapter on "Supporting inclusive education" (pp. 858–870) by Megan P. Martins, Sandra L. Harris, and Jan S. Handleman.

101    Some of the issues here are discussed by Andrew Fenton and Tim Krahn in their paper, "Autism, neurodiversity, and equality beyond the 'normal.' " *Journal of Ethics in Mental Health* 2, no. 2 (2007):1–6. One of the present authors attempts to show how and why discussions of autism should avoid the rhetoric of disease in Christopher Mole, "Autism and 'disease': The semantics of an ill-posed question." *Philosophical Psychology* 30, no. 8 (2017): 1126–1140.

102    One context in which words can be seen to matter in themselves is when we are trying to understand conditions that limit the intellectual achievements of children. A form of moral progress has been achieved by the movement towards a vocabulary of "Intellectual disability," and away from the previous vocabularies of "Mental retardation," or "Cretinism." This is progress that has been achieved partly through the words themselves, whether or not any substantial theoretical shift lay behind the verbal change. For a history of this change, see David Wright's 1996 discussion, " 'Childlike in his innocence': Lay attitudes to 'idiots' and 'imbeciles' in Victorian England", published in Anne Digby and David Wright (eds.) *From Idiocy to Mental Deficiency: Historical Perspectives on People with Learning Disabilities* (Routledge), 118–133. Other papers in that volume provide further context.

103    For discussion of the idea that the uniqueness of each patient is a barrier to their classification, and so to an evidence-based medicine of psychiatry, see Gloria Ayob's paper "Do people defy generalizations?: Examining the case against evidence-based medicine in psychiatry." *Philosophy, Psychiatry & Psychology* 15, no. 2 (2008): 167–174. For a discussion of the particular way in which

individual circumstances might figure in diagnoses of Major depressive disorder, particularly in the context of grief, see Şerife Tekin and Melissa Mosko's "Hyponarrativity and context-specific limitations of the DSM-5." *Public Affairs Quarterly* 29, no. 1 (2015): 111–136.

104   For the idea that the usefulness of our diagnostic categories is their whole point, and that no further question of accuracy need be asked, see George J. Agich's 2002 paper "Implications of a pragmatic theory of disease for the DSMs" published as Chapter Seven of John Z. Sadler (ed.) *Descriptions and Prescriptions: Values, Mental Disorders, and the DSMs* (Johns Hopkins University Press), 96–113. A somewhat similar idea can be found in Peter Zachar's article, "The practical kinds model as a pragmatist theory of classification." *Philosophy, Psychiatry & Psychology* 9, no. 3 (2002): 219–227.

105   One example of the public criticism of the motivations for revisions to the DSM's classificatory scheme can be found in Andrew Scull's article, "Nosologies," published in the 18 May 2012 edition of *The Times Literary Supplement*.

106   There certainly are ongoing debates about the foundations on which psychiatric categorizations are built. Matthew R. Broome reviews them in his paper, "Taxonomy and ontology in psychiatry: A survey of recent literature." *Philosophy, Psychiatry & Psychology* 13, no 4 (2006): 303–319.

107   Philosophers of science have been much concerned with the consequences of science's fitful and asymptotic approach to the truth, especially those philosophers of science who have been influenced by Karl Popper's seminal 1935 work on the logic of scientific discovery: *Logik der Forschung: Zur Erkenntnistheorie der Modernen Naturwissenschaft* (Springer), published in English in 1959 as *The Logic of Scientific Discovery* (Hutchinson).

108   For an in-depth consideration of the ways in the process of psychiatric diagnosis depends on features of context, and of the proper role for diagnostic classificatory systems, such as the DSM, within that process, see John Z. Sadler's 2005 book *Values and Psychiatric Diagnosis* (Oxford University Press). Sadler's concluding chapter is particularly relevant for understanding the handling of diagnoses, but the book as a whole provides an illuminating discussion of many of the issues that we are concerned with here.

109   The most complete discussion of the thinking about race that we are drawing on here is that given by Kwame Anthony Appiah and Amy Gutmann in their 1998 book, *Color Conscious: The Political Morality of Race* (Princeton University Press).

110   This history is recounted by Eric R. Scerri in his 2011 book, *The Periodic Table: A Very Short Introduction* (Oxford University Press).

111   An accessible introduction to several strands in Locke's thinking can be found in J.L. Mackie's 1976 book, *Problems from Locke* (Oxford University Press). Michael Ayer's 1991 *Locke: Epistemology and Ontology* (Routledge) shows how these strands are woven together, and situates them in their broader historical and philosophical contexts.

112   John Locke is depicted on p. 99 in a study of Sir Godfrey Kneller's 1697 Portrait.

113   Robert Boyle is depicted on p. 100 in a study of the portrait in Louis Figuier's 1867 *Les merveilles de la science, ou description populaire des inventions modernes* (Furne, Jouvet et Cie).

114   As we noted earlier, the idea that the periodic table might provide one model of a classificatory scheme to which psychiatry should aspire is discussed in Kenneth S. Kendler, Peter Zachar, and Carl Craver's "What kinds of things are psychiatric disorders?" *Psychological Medicine* 41, no 6 (2011): 1143–1150.

115   This point – which we elaborate in Chapter 3.3 – is central to the work of Ian Hacking. Those looking for a place to start with Hacking's incomparable body of work on philosophical aspects of mental disorder are advised to start with his 1995 book *Rewriting the Soul: Multiple Personality and the Sciences of Memory* (Princeton University Press). On the present point, few better things have been written than his 1986 paper, "Making up people," first published in *Reconstructing Individualism: Autonomy, Individuality, and the Self in Western Thought*, edited by Thomas Heller, Morton Sosna, and David E. Wellbery, (Stanford University Press), 222–236 and reprinted in 2002, as Chapter Six in a collection of Hacking's papers, *Historical Ontology* (Harvard University Press). An equally important and equally influential discussion can be found in Hacking's 1995 article "The looping effects of human kinds," first published in Dan Sperber, David Premack, and Ann J. Premack, (eds.) *Causal Cognition: A Multidisciplinary Debate* (Clarendon Press), 351–394.

116   The abandonment of Lockean aspirations, and the embrace of a pragmatic conception of our diagnostic categories, is advocated by Derek Bolton in his 2012 paper, "Classification and causal mechanisms: A deflationary approach to the classification problem," published in Kenneth S. Kendler and Josef Parnas (eds.), *Philosophical Issues in Psychiatry II: Nosology* (Oxford University Press), 6–11. Other contributions to this volume suggest a variety of different approaches to these issues.

117   The goldpanner depicted on p. 102 is drawn from a photograph of a 1935 prospector, published in the *Süddeutsche Zeitung*. (© Scherl/Süddeutsche Zeitung Photo, and reproduced here with their kind permission.)

# 3.2 Psychiatry Without Diagnostic Categories?

On several occasions in the history of psychiatry there have been resurgences of support for the idea that one or two broad categories should suffice for the classification of mental disorders. Differences between mentally disordered patients could then be attributed, not to different psychological disorders, but to differences in their personalities and circumstances.[118]

Like many ideas in psychiatry, this one had its origins in the German-speaking world. It is sometimes known by the German name of the *Einheitspsychosen* hypothesis: the hypothesis that mental disorders form a unified category – an *Einheit* – with any further divisions of that category being arbitrary.[119]

Although it does not deny the existence of psychiatric disorder, the *Einheitspsychosen* hypothesis might be thought to pose a threat to psychiatry's status as a science. This threat emerges when three ideas, none of which is threatening in itself, are combined. Each of these ideas is controversial, but each enjoys some plausibility. They are worth considering individually, before we consider the consequences of taking them together.

The first idea is that, in order to be properly scientific, an enquiry must be concerned with *explaining* things, where the explanation of a thing is understood to involve providing an account of the processes that cause this thing to come about.[120]

The second idea is that there is some real difference between causal processes and those sequences of events that are causally unrelated, with one part of this difference being that, whereas a causally unrelated sequence might happen anyhow, the happening of a causal process is governed by the laws of nature.[121]

The third idea is that laws of nature can apply to the items in some category only if that category is a natural one.[122] There might be laws that apply to all and only the negatively charged ions, or laws that apply to all and only the crows, but there are no laws – or, at least, no laws *of nature* – that apply to all and only the things in my pocket, or all and only the things that happen to be mentioned in the thirteenth edition of the *Encyclopædia Britannica*.

This last idea depends, in turn, on the thought that some ways of dividing up the world into categories are natural, whereas others are not. That thought is immediately appealing. It would be natural to categorize all the crows together in one group, with other birds in others. Different avian categorizations might be equally natural. We might group all the falcons into one group, all the gulls into another, and all the finches into a third, or we might group birds by their migratory habits, by their diets, or by their typical habitats. Any of these categorizations would be at least somewhat natural, but there are other ways of dividing up the set of birds that would, in contrast, be quite arbitrary. There would be nothing natural about a taxonomy that divided up the birds so that one category contains all and only those birds that have been alive for an odd number of days, and another contains all and only those that have been alive for an even number of days. Nor would it be natural to divide up the birds on the basis of whether they happen to have been mentioned in the *Encyclopædia Britannica,* or depicted in the poetry of Wallace Stevens.

We could categorize birds in these last arbitrary ways if we wanted to. There might even be some esoteric purposes for which the resulting categorizations would be useful. But such categorizations would not be "cutting nature at its joints." We should be wary of treating this distinction between natural and unnatural categories as if it were sharp. It is nonetheless true that some classificatory schemes do seem to be more natural than others, and that this difference between groupings seems to relate, in some way, to the distinction between the laws of nature and those un-law-like generalizations that merely happen to be true.

To see this last connection, notice that it is because crows form a natural kind that the generalization saying that all crows are black can be thought of as something like a law of nature. Perhaps it is not a very important or fundamental law, but it does at least seem to be more like a law than like a coincidence. This contrasts with any generalization that might happen to be true of all those birds that are an odd number of days old, or with any generalization that might happen to be true of all those birds that figure in the poetry of Wallace Stevens. It would be strange to think that there is any law of nature specifying that every bird mentioned in Wallace Stevens' poetry is black, even if that generalization turns out to be no less true than the generalization about the blackness of crows. Even if it does happen to be true, the generalization about birds that figure in Wallace Stevens' poetry seems like a matter of how things turn out to have been – perhaps by chance, or perhaps as a consequence of Stevens' own idiosyncratic tastes. Generalizations about the category of *crows* seem more law-like, and more dependent on the nature of things.

This difference of law-likeness gives rise to a difference of explanatory potential. We can cite the generalization saying that all crows are black in the course of *explaining why* some particular bird – such as the one that is now sitting on my chimney pot – is black: That bird is black because it is a crow, and because all crows are black. We cannot give an explanation for that crow's blackness by citing any generalizations about the poetry in which this bird is depicted. If we are being asked for an explanation, it will not do to say that the bird on my chimney pot is black because Wallace Stevens wrote a poem about it. Because the generalization about Wallace Stevens' poetry is not a law – but is just a matter of how things happen to be – the citing of it cannot do explanatory work, of the sort that scientific theories aspire to do.[123]

Although none of them is uncontentious, each of the three ideas that we have just outlined is plausible. Combining them gives us the controversial result that no enquiry can be properly scientific if the categories with which it operates are arbitrary or unnatural (and combining this, in turn, with the *Einheitspsychosen* hypothesis makes trouble for the scientific status of psychiatry).

We can see that this result follows logically from these three ideas, by taking them in reverse order: If an enquiry's categories are arbitrary then the generalizations about those categories are not law like (this was idea three). If the generalizations are not law like then they cannot figure in causal explanations (this was idea two). And if causal explanations cannot be given when using these generalizations, then the practice in which those generalizations are identified cannot be properly scientific (this was idea one). The scientific status of an enquiry therefore seems to depend upon the non-arbitrary status of its categories.

The conclusion of this line of thought can, if it is right, be applied to all sorts of human sciences.[124] The consequences of its application are, in general, pessimistic, and the line of thought is, as a result, controversial. It should therefore be treated with suspicion. But if this line of thought is applicable to the case of psychiatry then it can be used to explain why the status of psychiatry's diagnostic categories has so often been contentious, and why there has been relatively little enthusiasm for the idea that we might give up on any attempt to identify such categories, and instead take mental disorder as a single *Einheit*, with the division of this into categories being more or less arbitrary. Unless some flaw is identified in the above line of thought, such arbitrariness would threaten psychiatry's claim to being scientific.

# Notes to Chapter 3.2

118    A recent report by "The Brainstorm Consortium" – a large group of researchers into psychiatric and neurological disorders – finds that patients with various psychiatric diagnosis seem to show similar patterns of genetic markers. It concludes:

> The high degree of genetic correlation among many of the psychiatric disorders adds further evidence that their current clinical boundaries do not reflect distinct underlying pathogenic processes, at least on the genetic level. This suggests a deeply interconnected nature for psychiatric disorders, in contrast to neurological disorders, and underscores the need to refine psychiatric diagnostics.

This 2018 report from the Brainstorm Consortium is published in *Science* 360, no. 6395, under the title "Analysis of shared heritability in common disorders of the brain." There is one interpretation of these results in which they can be thought of as reviving the prospects for something like the *Einheitspsychosen* hypothesis, as discussed in this chapter.

119    Examples of other work in which something like the *Einheitspsychosen* hypothesis has been advocated can be found in:

Robert E. Kendell. "The major functional psychoses: Are they independent entities or part of a continuum? Philosophical and conceptual issues underlying the debate." in *Concepts of Mental Disorder A Continuing Debate* (Gaskell), 1–16, edited by Alan Kerr and Hamish McClelland.

Nick Craddock and Michael J. Owen. "The beginning of the end for the Kraepelinian dichotomy." *British Journal of Psychiatry* 186, no. 5 (2005): 364–366.

Juan J. Lopez-Ibor and Maria-Ines Lopez-Ibor. "Paving the way for new research strategies in mental disorders. First part: The recurring crisis of psychiatry." *Actas Española de Psiquiatría* 41, no. 1: 33–43.

120    One of the reasons why science cannot avoid being in the business of giving explanations is that scientific reasoning very often proceeds by inference to the *best* explanation. Our evidence almost never entails that our theories must be true. Instead, the evidence makes a theory plausible because that theory enables us to give a clear explanation for it. Gilbert Harman gives an important argument for the idea that explanations play an essential role in all sorts of scientific reasoning (and in all other sorts of reasoning, except for the strictly deductive reasoning used in logic and mathematics) in his 1965 paper "The

inference to the best explanation." *Philosophical Review* 74, no 1 (1965): 88–95. Peter Lipton considers the issues in depth in his 2004 book *Inference to the Best Explanation* (Routledge).

121   In Part One we saw that philosophers have been suspicious of the distinction between causal processes and sets of events that merely happen to take place in sequence, without any causal relations between them. They have been similarly suspicious of the distinction between laws of nature and generalizations that merely happen to be true across a range of instances. On meeting these puzzles, it is natural to think that they might somehow be related, so that one of the distinctions can be used to illuminate the other. For a thorough introduction to the idea that causal processes are, essentially, governed by laws of nature, see John W. Carroll's 1994 book, *Laws of Nature* (Cambridge University Press).

122   For a variety of philosophical perspectives on the idea that some taxonomies succeed in employing categories that correspond to groupings that are independently present in nature, see the essays collected in Joseph Keim Campbell, Michael O'Rourke, and Matthew H. Slater, (eds.) *Carving Nature at its Joints: Natural Kinds in Metaphysics and Science* (MIT Press, 2011).

123   The controversial ideas that we are working with here have been at the center of some long-standing philosophical disputes about the nature of scientific explanation, and about the role of laws in it. The modern phase of these disputes begins with Carl G. Hempel and Paul Oppenheim's "Studies in the logic of explanation." *Philosophy of Science* 15, no. 2 (1948): 135–175. For some recent contributions to these disputes, see Garrett Pendergraft, "In defense of a causal requirement on explanation," published in Phyllis McKay Illari, Federica Russo, and Jon Williamson (eds.) *Causality in the Sciences* (Oxford University Press, 2011), 470–493. Other papers in the same volume also provide a number of sophisticated analyses of ideas that are central to the issues discussed in the present chapter.

124   Ruth Millikan examines one way in which the generalized version of this line of thought might be resisted, in her "Historical kinds and the 'special sciences'." *Philosophical Studies* 95, no. 1–2 (1999): 45–65. For an alternative way of rejecting some of the ideas that generate the problem we are setting out here, see Jonathan Cohen and Craig Callender's "Special sciences, conspiracy and the better best system account of lawhood." *Erkenntnis* 73, no. 3 (2010): 427–447.

## 3.3 Categories Unlike Chemistry's

It would be a false dichotomy to suppose that psychiatry must either be operating with pre-existing groupings, which exist independently of us and which are analogous to chemistry's grouping of elements by atomic number, or else must be operating with groupings that are merely arbitrary, and that are therefore analogous to the grouping of people by their stereotypical race, or of birds by the quantity of American symbolist poetry that has been written about them.[125]

The point here is not just that some groupings fall in the middle of a continuum between the natural and the arbitrary. The picture in which all groupings fall on a single dimension of naturalness is only slightly less simplistic than the picture in which all groupings fall into one or the other of these categories. The point is just that different groupings operate quite differently, not that they fall on any one continuum.

Some groupings might emerge in the course of our classificatory work (and so not be pre-existing or independent). Having emerged, those groupings might then take on a life of their own, so that the relevant classifications really *do* apply to people (with the result that they are not illusory).

We can see a relatively uncontroversial instance of this if we consider the cultural identities of young adults. Consider the examples of the Dandy, the Hipster, the Crusty, the New Romantic, the Goth, the Punk, the Mod, the Emo, and the Beatnik.[126]

Each of these categories has its own stereotype, but none of them is *merely* a stereotype. These classifications really do, or did, apply to people. There really have been goths, hipsters, and all the rest. When anthropologists of the distant future say that there were once hipsters, they will be saying something that is perfectly correct, however implausible it might then seem.

These groups typically predate the names by which they come to be known. There were hipsters before the name "hipster" had been coined, and beatniks before anyone had thought of that term. (The goths are a more complicated case.) Although the groups with which young adults affiliate themselves typically predate their naming, none of those groups exists independently of the categorization practices in which those names are applied. Such groups emerge from our tendency to apply categorizations to ourselves and to one another, and from our tendency to use such categorizations when making sense of our own and one another's behavior.

These tendencies operate to produce and sustain the subcultures of young adulthood, but they are not tendencies on which young adults have any monopoly. The same tendencies can also interact with any of the innumerable other things that are taken into consideration when we are engaged in the business of understanding ourselves and one another. They figure, alongside other factors, in the explanation of why it is that husbands act like husbands, waiters act like waiters, and doctors act like doctors.[127]

These same tendencies continue to operate when the categories in question are ones that we do not choose for ourselves: whereas most waiters are waiters voluntarily, and most husbands choose to be husbands, it is not the case that younger sisters choose to be sisters, nor that uncles choose to be uncles. It is nonetheless true that the sisterly behavior of sisters and the avuncular behavior of uncles seem partly to be explained by the fact that these people think of themselves as belonging to these categories, and then go on to form expectations for themselves based on a set of culturally derived expectations about the way in which the members of those categories typically behave. Other factors will also be at work in any particular case, but this pattern of more or less benign self-stereotyping seems to be at least part of the explanation for some of the things that go on in our lives.

The same tendencies continue to operate when we are thinking about mental health and mental disorder. They might therefore make some contribution to the explanation of why it is that patients act as they do, and – more specifically – to the explanation of why it is that anxious patients, obsessive patients, and depressed patients act in the anxious, obsessive, and depressed ways that they do. Our tendencies for group conformity and self-stereotyping are, of course, not the only contributor to the explanations of these behaviors. Their contribution here may be very much smaller than it is in the case of young adult sub-cultures, but it nonetheless seems likely that *some* such contribution is made.

It will be difficult to find a position from which to gauge the extent of that contribution. A patient's own perspective may be especially ill-suited to the gauging of it, just as the hipster may be in a poor position to judge the extent to which his tastes have been shaped by the cultural identity that he is enacting.

This hipster may sincerely assert that the need to fit in with his peers has nothing to do with his choices, and that he really does, independently, have a liking for full beards, retro tattoos, vinyl records, and cold-brewed coffee. The Marxists would diagnose a case of false consciousness, but there is no reason to suppose that our hipster is *mistaken* about his preferences. The point is just that he is not in an especially good position to ascertain the way in which those preferences have formed.

Our tendencies to create stereotypical groupings – and to use the language of such groupings when thinking about ourselves and others – can easily create self-fulfilling prophecies, based on group conformity. On finding some person to be a hipster, we expect that he will grow a beard. And thinking of himself as being the sort of person who might typically grow a beard, this hipster then becomes more likely to grow one. Not every prophecy fulfills itself, and not every hipsterish trait is prophesized. The mechanism of group conformity does not explain all of the hipster's characteristics. No doubt the situation is a good deal more complicated in the psychiatric case. But in cases of both sorts there is the possibility for the mechanisms of self-fulfilling prophecy, based on group identification, to be at work.

Take, for a psychiatric example, the condition that was previously diagnosed as "Seasonal affective disorder," and that is now known as "Major depressive disorder, recurrent, with seasonal pattern."

If some person has been diagnosed with a condition that they believe will typically fluctuate over the course of the year, we might then expect this person to become increasingly pessimistic as the evenings get darker. If the person thinks of himself in these terms, he might then be more likely to feel pessimistic at that time of year. And this expectation might itself make some contribution to his becoming depressed in the darker months, thereby confirming that very expectation. A similar mechanism – similar also to the mechanisms of group identification that make hipsters more or less likely to buy vinyl records, drink cold-brewed coffee, and grow beards – might contribute to the opposite change in the springtime.[128] A well-established line of feminist thought emphasizes the fact that these self-fulfilling expectations can often be antithetical to our flourishing.[129] Again it should be emphasized that other forces are, of course, at work, but again it can be hard to gauge how much should be attributed to the force of conformity with expectations that are formed on the basis of identifying with some group.

One of the reasons why the influence of culture can be hard to gauge in the psychiatric case is that, whether or not a patient's symptoms show the influence of that patient's culture, some cultural influence is very likely to be seen in the way in which this patient gives her account of what those symptoms are.[130] Cultural factors will therefore influence the patient's *explanation* for their symptoms, whether or not they influence the symptoms themselves. They will also influence the patient's understanding of the things that are appropriately mentioned in a psychiatric setting. The reinforcing effects of expectations may then be exacerbated in the case of psychiatric diagnoses, just because this particular diagnostic process typically requires patients to give an account of themselves.

Because self-fulfilling prophecies create positive feedback loops, they can be susceptible to sudden change, both in their development and in their decline. We see this in a range of self-reinforcing cultural phenomena. Rubik's cubes, moustaches, and skinny lattes[131] are suddenly everywhere, and then somehow they disappear, surviving in only a few die-hard groups, with the resulting cultural vacuum eventually being filled by fidget-spinners, full beards, and cold-brewed coffee. Some mental disorders have shown a similar profile of sudden emergence, followed by a process of comparably sudden decline.

Dissociative identity disorder (or Multiple personality disorder, as it was once known) is a noted case of this. There seem always to have been some cases of multiple personality, but in the 1980s the diagnosis of Multiple personality disorder surged dramatically. This sudden prevalence provoked a great deal of controversy regarding its possible causes, until the number of cases reported in the literature suddenly fell off. The condition is now diagnosed only rarely.[132]

The sudden way in which such disorders emerge, and then all-but disappear, is not the only indication that socially mediated positive feedback loops might play a role in their occurrence. The distribution of these disorders across different cultures also points in the same direction.

There are certain recognizable motifs that recur in scattered cases in the histories of mental disorder, against a variety of cultural backgrounds, and that then take on a life of their own, against a cultural background that seems to be especially conducive to their development. Disorders of eating and of body image are one example. If we look across a broad range of historical and social settings then, in a variety of these cultural contexts, we can find occasional cases of what seem to be eating disorders. The cultural context found in the turn-of-the-millennium West seems to have been exceptionally conducive to the development of such disorders. Since cultures that had known nothing of Anorexia nervosa have begun to display cases of it, just as the influence of Western culture comes to be felt in them, it seems to be that culture is one crucial factor in precipitating the temporal and geographical extent of this epidemic.[133]

Different cultures seem prone to producing disorders of other sorts. The writings of Freud and his contemporaries give the impression that their patients rather frequently displayed the symptoms of hysterical paralysis, or hysterical blindness.[134] If this was indeed the case then it may have been that Viennese society at the turn of the twentieth century was especially prone to the development of those particular symptoms. Such symptoms are not unheard of in current practice, but nor are they at all commonplace. Other cultures are a source of other examples. In many but not all Chinese cultures there is a recognized disorder that involves a delusional belief that one's penis is shrinking into one's abdomen, and that this will result in death. Such delusions are sometimes encountered in other cultures, but only rarely. In some but not all Japanese cultures there is a recognized disorder that involves a preoccupation with the idea that one's body smells offensively. Again it is true that similar conditions can be found in other cultural contexts, but again these are manifested in a somewhat different way. In the present mainstream of North American culture we find some evidence indicating that the content of delusions can be shaped by themes that are prevalent in contemporary media and film.[135] Cultural models also seem to affect the experience of medically unexplained symptoms, and of hypochondriacal worry.[136] In all of these cases it would seem that socially mediated expectations are making some contribution to the way in which disordered thinking takes shape, and so to the way in which it manifests itself in the lives of those who suffer from it.[137]

If people ceased to think of themselves as goths, hipsters, beatniks, and all the rest, then the world would become a less interesting place. People would still need to find ways to be distinctively themselves, and to signal their cultural affiliations, but they might not go to the same lengths in doing so. Because positive feedback loops reinforce themselves, the people who do think of themselves as belonging to categories can become more likely to display extreme forms of traits that would otherwise be normally distributed.

In the case of psychiatric diagnoses, the extremities begotten by these feedback loops are less benign. If people ceased to think of themselves as bipolar, compulsive, impulsive, and all the rest, they would still need to find ways in which to manifest and conceptualize the disorderliness of their lives, but they might not go to the same lengths in doing so. Seeing themselves categorized as bipolar, as obsessive, or as impulsive might make some contribution to the manifestation of disorder in each case. It should also be remembered, however, that there are cases in which the awareness that comes with such self-categorization might mitigate the trouble that a disorder causes: It is not unusual for people to report a sense of relief on learning that they are not alone in suffering from some psychiatric condition, and on finding that there is a community of people who identify the same condition as a part of their experience.

# Notes to Chapter 3.3

125   S. Nassir Ghaemi provides a critique of the idea that we should take a merely pragmatic approach to psychiatry's diagnostic categories in his 2012 paper "Taking disease seriously: Beyond 'pragmatic' nosology", published in Kenneth S. Kendler and Josef Parnas (eds.), *Philosophical Issues in Psychiatry II: Nosology* (Oxford University Press, 2012), 42–72. Ghaemi relates the philosophical issues here to some of the particular debates concerning ways in which the taxonomic approach taken by the DSM has changed, over the course of its several revisions.

126   The goths depicted on this chapter's first page are Marchesa Luisa Casati and a friend, photographed in Paris, in 1910, by an unknown photographer.

127   The example of waiters who act like waiters plays a important role in Jean Paul Sartre's *L'être et le néant* (*Being and Nothingness*) (Gallimard). Our treatment of the present point owes something to the existentialist philosophy that Sartre articulated.

128   The mood-lowering effects of expectations regarding a low mood are real enough, but the role of cultural norms and variations in seasonal changes of mood also seems to involve a number of very much more complicated factors. For discussion of these, see Joseph Kasof's paper, "Cultural variation in seasonal depression: Cross-national differences in winter versus summer patterns of seasonal affective disorder." *Journal of Affective Disorders* 115, no. 1 (2009): 79–86.

The mood-changing effects of atmospheric conditions can be seen, not only in the experience of people prone to depression, but also in the fluctuations of financial markets. William N. Goetzman, Dasol Kim, Alok Kumar, and Qin Wang provide evidence for this in their paper "Weather-induced mood, institutional investors, and stock returns," published in *The Review of Financial Studies* 28, no. 1 (2015): 73–111.

129   Judith Butler has developed an influential line of thinking concerning the ways in which social expectations play out in our lives, and about the ways in which we might emancipate ourselves from the limitations that these impose, with particular reference to the expectations associated with gender. Her 1997 book, *Excitable Speech: A Politics of the Performative* (Routledge), explores this in detail. Marilyn Frye's work, considering the numerous ways in which expectations can conspire to invisibly limit the ways of living that a person recognizes as possible, also throws valuable light on a number of the issues in this area, as these arise in connection to gender, race, and sexuality. The essays collected in

her 1983 book, *The Politics of Reality* (Crossing Press), develop a strong critique of such limitations.

130 Jeremy Holmes discusses the crucial role that is played in psychiatry by the patient's own account of their condition in his article, "Narrative in psychiatry and psychotherapy: The evidence?" *Medical Humanities* 26, no. 2 (2000): 92–96.

131 Jonathan Morris discusses the social factors contributing to the spread of coffee preferences in his article "Why espresso? Explaining changes in European coffee preferences from a production of culture perspective." *European Review of History: Revue européenne d'histoire* 20, no. 5 (2013): 881–901.

132 The degree of controversy surrounding Dissociative identity disorder, and the decline in its diagnosis, can be seen by contrasting August Piper and Harold Merskey's paper "The persistence of folly: A critical examination of Dissociative identity disorder. Part I. The excesses of an improbable concept." *The Canadian Journal of Psychiatry* 49, no. 9 (2004): 592–600, and a paper by A. A. T. Simone Reinders, Antoon T. M. Willemsen, Herry P. J. Vos, Johan A. den Boer, and Ellert R. S. Nijenhuis: "Fact or factitious? A psychobiological study of authentic and simulated Dissociative identity states." *PLoS* One 7, no. 6 (2012): e39279.

133 The evidence for the role of Western acculturation in the spread of Anorexia nervosa is not unequivocal. It is reviewed, and the limitations of it are discussed, in Eli Doris, Ia Shekriladze, Nino Javakhishvili, Roshan Jones, Janet Treasure, and Kate Tchanturia, "Is cultural change associated with eating disorders? A systematic review of the literature." *Eating and Weight Disorders-Studies on Anorexia, Bulimia and Obesity* 20, no. 2 (2015): 149–160.

134 Freudian diagnoses of hysteria were mainstream for much of the twentieth century. An explicitly Freudian account of hysteria affecting the visual system can be found in a 1915 article, entitled "A case of hysterical amblyopia," and published in *The British Medical Journal* 2, no. 2855: 434. The author is Kenneth Campbell. For a discussion, from within the Freudian wing of psychology, of the disappearance of such cases, see Roberta Satow's paper, "Where has all the hysteria gone?" *Psychoanalytic Review* 66, no. 4 (1979): 463–477.

The nature and explanation of the decline in hysterical symptoms is discussed in Hiroko Akagi and Allan House's article "The clinical epidemiology of hysteria: Vanishingly rare, or just vanishing?" *Psychological Medicine* 32, no. 2 (2002): 191–194.

For a discussion of our current understanding of such bodily symptoms as Freud would have characterized as hysterical, see the paper by Peter Henningsen, Thorsten Jakobsen, Marcus Schiltenwolf, and Mitchell G. Weiss. "Somatization revisited: Diagnosis and perceived causes of common mental disorders." *The Journal of Nervous and Mental Disease* 193, no. 2 (2005): 85–92.

135  For a recent example in which mental disorder can be seen to reflect ideas from the culture at large, see Joel Gold and Ian Gold's paper "The 'Truman Show' delusion: Psychosis in the global village." *Cognitive Neuropsychiatry* 17, no. 6 (2012): 455–472.

136  Laurence J. Kirmayer and Norman Sartorius discuss a number of diverse cultural influences on experiences of, and interpretation of, unexplained bodily symptoms in their article, "Cultural models and somatic syndromes." *Psychosomatic Medicine* 69, no. 9 (2007): 832–840.

## 3.4 Giving the Brain No More Than Its Due

We have seen that a classificatory scheme might lead people to think of themselves as belonging to categories that then become self-reinforcing, whether or not the scheme has any independent grounding. We have seen that these mechanisms of self-reinforcement might sometimes exacerbate a person's problems.[137] We have also seen that there are questions to be answered about whether psychiatry's current classificatory scheme is a case of this. These include questions about whether assigning people to psychiatric categories might sometimes exacerbate their problems, and questions about the basis on which the distinctions between those categories have been drawn. Even the most ardent advocates of psychiatry's current classificatory scheme think that the process of revising and refining it is unfinished. Rather than persisting with such revisionary work, there are many theorists who would like to throw out this current scheme, in the hope of then starting afresh.[138]

The fresh start that they hope for is one that builds on the basis of observations that can be made using various technologies for gauging the anatomy of brains, and for measuring the activities that are taking place inside them. Many of these technologies were unavailable at the time when psychiatry's existing classificatory schemes were devised. Some were unimaginable.

These hopes for a fresh taxonomic start are motivated, not only by the existence of new technologies for observing the brain and its activities, but also by the development of computationally sophisticated methods for processing the data that such technologies give to us. These are methods that draw on recent developments in artificial intelligence, and, more specifically, on the branch of artificial intelligence that is concerned with machine learning. Computational systems that use machine learning have been shown to do a remarkably good job of classifying images, texts, and videos. One of their many recent applications has been in medical diagnosis, where they have been found to improve on the performance of expert humans, in some image-based diagnostic tasks.[139]

These successes raise the question of whether the tasks of psychiatric diagnosis might be among those to which new technologies could be applied. This question is currently a topic of active research. If the computer scientists' latest methods can indeed be applied to the data that come from scanning the brains of people in various states of mental health and mental disorder, then the results that come from these methods might change our diagnostic and therapeutic practices in any number of ways. They might suggest new ways to classify mental disorders. They might also enable us to find new ways in which those disorders can be treated.

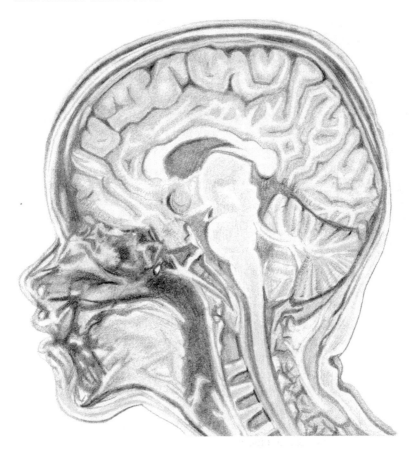

The attempt to use these technologies to facilitate a freshly brain-centered approach to the taxonomy of psychiatry is currently being pursued in the United States, by the National Institute for Mental Health, and by other prominent research institutions.[140] It also has advocates elsewhere in the anglophone world.[141]

The advantages that new technology promises are, in some cases, clear. Advances in our understanding of genetics and epigenetics promise to lead to the discovery of new treatments for mental disorders,[142] and they promise to streamline the process of finding treatments that work, with minimal complications, for individual patients.[143] But even if the new generation of high-tech methods does lead to the creation of reliable new procedures for prescribing psychiatric drug treatments, on the basis of information about each patient's brain, the development of such procedures might not put psychiatrists out of a job. Humans might retain their role in those parts of psychiatric treatment that include therapeutic conversation. Even here, however, there are technological developments that might bring about changes. Some disorders might come to be treated in ways that involve conversation, not with a human therapist, but with a fully automated app, or with some other computational system. There is a relatively long history of attempts to build such systems.

The early attempts to write computer programs that could engage in therapeutic conversations were rather less successful than is sometimes suggested,[144] but a number of new programs are currently in development.[145] One recent program – the "Woebot" – is a chatbot that lives in the online environment of an instant messaging app. It can administer a version of Cognitive Behavioral Therapy. A preliminary trial suggests that it has some success in countering anxious and depressive symptoms.[146]

Whether or not computational systems come to have any role in the prescription of drugs for mental disorders, or in the administration of talking therapies for them, it seems that the *diagnosis* of these disorders might be subject to technologically driven change. The removal of humans from psychiatry's diagnostic process would be a mixed blessing. Some psychiatric treatments might be effective partly because they are given from a position of human understanding.[147] The event of being listened to, and of having one's condition understood, can itself contribute to recovery, even before the psychiatrist reaches any diagnostic verdict, or suggests any particular course of treatment. These advantages would be lost in the move toward diagnoses that are made wholly by a computer, especially if those diagnoses were made on the basis of data from the brain, rather than being made on the basis of a person's own account of their experiences.

Other changes that might come from these technological developments could be more positive. Some patients might be more receptive to a diagnosis that has been made by a dispassionate algorithm, rather than by a person. Consider, for example, the diagnosis of Histrionic personality disorder, which is characterized by "a pervasive pattern of excessive emotionality and attention seeking." Coming from a person to whom one has recounted the problems of one's life, such a diagnosis might seem to be impertinently judgmental. A diagnosis that is given as the dispassionate output of a computation – and not as a direct human appraisal – might, in some cases, have the advantage of avoiding any such connotation.[148]

Whether it would, on balance, be a good or bad thing, the idea of an artificially intelligent system for diagnosing psychiatric patients is presently no more than science fiction. The question of whether it is destined to remain fictional is a difficult one. There is a long tradition of philosophers arguing that computers must inevitably fail to perform certain tasks. There is an equally well established tradition of computer scientists showing these philosophical arguments to be mistaken, by succeeding in just the ways that the philosophers thought would be impossible. Computational systems that play world-class chess and Go arrived much sooner than philosophers thought would be possible.[149] So too did computational systems that do an adequate job of translating between different human languages. In some branches of medicine outside of psychiatry, computational methods for diagnosis have already proven to be far better than might have been expected, even when performing tasks that were previously thought to require human expertise.[150]

Without making any predictions that might join the ranks of those that have been falsified by the accelerating rate of technological developments, we want to suggest that there might be some reasons to doubt that we will soon have fully computerized machines, in which reliable psychiatric diagnoses can be made on the basis of information that is drawn entirely from technologies for observing the brain. (In the discussion that follows we use the term "brain scan" to refer to such technologies, meaning when we do so to include the full range of present and future methods for probing the structure and function of the brain, including neuroimaging methods and the methods of electroencephalography.)

Our reasons to be sceptical develop some of the earlier themes of this book. It was a theme in Part Two of this book that social factors have more than one role to play in the explanation of mental disorders, by contributing to bringing about some conditions, and by contributing to some of those conditions being disorderly. Brain-scan-based diagnostic machines could take account of these social factors only insofar as they are factors that leave discernable traces in the brain. If social factors leave no such traces, then methods of diagnosis that are based only on brain scans would inevitably be blind to them. A brain-scanning enthusiast might think that this limitation of brain scanning could not possibly be of any clinical significance: Anything that influences a brain's functioning must make *some* difference to that brain. It follows from this that those social factors that make no difference in the brain could not possibly be playing any immediate role in the explanation of that brain's functioning. It therefore seems that such factors cannot be playing any immediate role in the disorderliness of a mind.[151] Although a brain-scan-based diagnostic method would be blind to those social factors that leave no traces in the brain, it can seem that any such factors would be ones to which that method can afford to be blind, since blindness to them could not possibly impair its diagnostic performance.

There are, however, reasons to be suspicious of the brain-scan enthusiasts' argument here. The remaining parts of our discussion try to bring these reasons to light. They take us back to some of the questions that we left unanswered in Part One of this book, when we asked how it is possible for there to be such things as genuinely *mental* disorders, given that every mental occurrence must have some basis in the physical and biochemical processes of the brain. Our discussion has now arrived at the point where we are able to see a way in which that question might be answered. Seeing this will enable us to see that there would be significant difficulties for any system that attempted to make psychiatric diagnoses only on the basis of data from brain scans, however much of that data was available.

The line of thought that is offered by our brain-scanning enthusiast suggests that, since the immediate causes of behavior, thought, and emotion must always be brain-based, a person's social context can be of immediate explanatory importance only if it leaves some trace in that person's brain. It concludes that nothing therapeutically relevant would be lost if we considered *only* the brain, without its social context. But this is an uncomfortable conclusion to have reached. The contexts to which our diagnostic machine would be blind do seem to be important in a range of cases. We have seen, in the earlier parts of this book, that we would likely need to make reference to social facts in order to explain the rise and fall of hysterical paralysis, of Anorexia nervosa, and of Dissociative identity disorder. We have also seen reasons to think that we would need to acknowledge a role for social facts, in giving a full explanation for the disorderliness of conditions like Tourette's disorder, Autism spectrum disorder, and Attention deficit hyperactivity disorder (ADHD).

Even in those mental disorders where social facts play a less obvious role, they do still seem to be playing *some* role, and so there would seem to be costs associated with the attempt to make our diagnoses without looking outside of the brain. This can be seen by considering the observation that one's risk of developing Schizophrenia increases in conditions of social isolation and displacement.[152] All sorts of facts about a socially isolated person's relationships and experiences might be relevant to this increase in risk, including facts that have their basis outside of that person's skull, and that no brain scan could bring into view. The statistical evidence that indicates the importance of these facts is on a sound scientific footing. We should prefer to avoid the conclusion that crediting them with importance is merely some pre-scientific prejudice. But our difficulty, in the face of the brain-scanning enthusiast's argument, is to see how that conclusion can possibly be avoided.

The issues that we are coming up against here relate to some broader issues concerning the status of *reductionism*, as a tactic in scientific explanation. Sometimes "reductive" explanations look to be the only sort of explanation that could possibly be scientific. That is because scientific reasoning very often proceeds by inferring that some theory must be correct, on the grounds that this theory provides the best explanation for certain phenomena.[153] The *best* explanations are judged, in the context of such inferences, to be those that exhibit a unifying simplicity. One result of this is that increases in scientific understanding will tend to progress towards the giving of explanations in ever simpler and more general terms. "Reductionism" can therefore seem to be an inevitable concomitant of scientific reasoning. There are other occasions, however, when the term "reductionism" is used in such a way that the commitment to reductionism seems like a commitment to narrow-mindedness. On these occasions "reductionist" is used as a term of abuse, suggesting a refusal to acknowledge the broad complexities that we know must be taken into account, if our explanations are to have any chance of being complete. The difficulties that we are facing here are the difficulties of determining whether an insistence on brain-based psychiatric diagnoses is reductionist in a good sense, or reductionist in a bad one.

We can begin to see a way through these difficulties by noticing that, although scientifically respectable explanations should avoid postulating outside influences in cases where internal forces would suffice, the scientific respectability of a theory has never required that theory to be given with reference only to the component parts of the things whose behavior we are trying to explain.

Consider, for a celebrated example, Isaac Newton's explanation of the planetary orbits.[154] Newton's achievement was to explain the planets' orbits by deducing them from a single set of laws, which are powerful enough to apply to all sorts of things, large or small, whatever the parts from which those things are made. The parts of the different planets are chemically quite different from one another. The explanations for the shape and timing of their orbits are nonetheless the same. If "reductionist" explanations are supposed to focus on component parts, rather than wholes, then Newton's explanation is not reductionist: It does *not* explain the orbits by focussing on the local properties of each planet's parts.[155] No explanation has ever been more scientifically respectable than Newton's. There is, therefore, a sense in which respectable science need not be reductionist.

The lesson to be drawn from the example of Newton is that a commitment to scientific reasoning does not incur any obligation to focus only on component parts.[156] It would therefore be a mistake to suppose that a scientific approach to mental disorders requires us to give explanations of those disorders solely by reference to the brain cells and neurotransmitters that are the component parts of a disordered brain. In this particular sense of "reductionism," the scientific approach taken by psychiatry does not require it to be reductionist.

But although a scientific approach does not require us to talk only about the parts from which a brain is made – and so does not immediately oblige us to prefer diagnostic methods that ignore social facts – it does require that, when seeking to explain mental disorders, we give our explanation without needlessly postulating any extraneous things, forces, or laws. It therefore requires that we prefer explanations that make reference to only a small number of things, and to only a small number of laws governing the behavior of those things. Again the Newtonian theory is an exemplar of this. Before Newton, the explanation of the planetary orbits was thought to require different laws from those governing the motion of things on Earth. After Newton, we could see that the same laws of motion operate in both spheres.

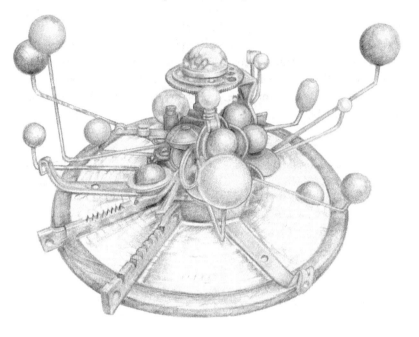

From this better-motivated version of reductionism, our original problem might still seem to arise. A brain is not made from anything other than things to which the laws of physics apply. Those laws aspire to being complete. Any extra-physical laws invoked by psychiatry therefore seem to be destined for redundancy. And so the psychiatrists' generalizations begin to seem like they must merely be place-holders, indicating points at which our understanding of the mind is waiting to be replaced by some more comprehensive theory of the physical events taking place in the brain. It therefore begins to seem that a complete science would have no place for any distinctively psychiatric level of explanation: A science of mental health that is based wholly on the information that can be gleaned from brain scanning begins to look like a step towards a science in which all distinctively psychological explanations have been replaced.

This brings us back to the problem that we met in the first parts of this book: If the explanations for a person's behavior are given in any vocabulary other than the language of physics, they can be made to seem like mere shadow explanations, with the real work being accomplished elsewhere.

This problem looks to be a severe one, as it did when we encountered it before. It seems to be a problem for every scientist except the physicist. The psychiatrist might take some comfort from the thought that it is not a special problem for the science of psychiatry. But to say this is not yet to solve the problem. One can be in good company while still being in trouble.

To find a way out of this problem, we need to make sense of the idea that something other than a brain's intrinsic physical properties can contribute to the mental disorderliness that is based in that brain. We need to make sense of this without postulating any extra-physical forces, of a sort that would be scientifically mysterious, and that would therefore be anathema to reductionism, in the good sense of that problematic word.

With this goal before us, it might sound disreputable to say that some physical objects have properties that are not derived from their physical properties, or to say that these properties can contribute to the disorderliness of those objects' behavior. But, provided that these claims are understood correctly, they need not be committed to the existence of anything that lies mysteriously, or irreducibly, beyond the physical realm.

We can begin to see this by seeing that these claims have some perfectly quotidian instances. Consider, for one very simple example, a bottle cap that might be sitting on the second rank of a chess board.[157] It – unlike some physically similar bottle caps that might also be found on the table – has been endowed with the property of being a pawn. Any number of physically various things can have that property. Several pieces of turned wood have it, as, elsewhere, do countless pieces of stone, metal, plastic, glass, and other physically and chemically various things. The philosopher Wilfrid Sellars once remarked that in Texas, where the land is flat and the fields are square, they can even play chess with Cadillacs.[158]

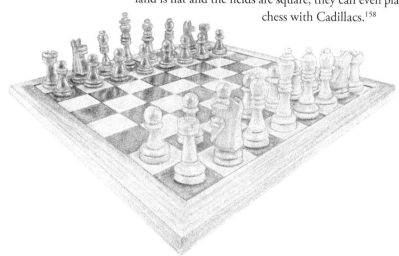

Things that are physically quite unlike this bottle cap can share its property of being a pawn. And things that are physically very similar to the bottle cap can lack that same property. It therefore seems that this particular property – the property of being a pawn – is not derived from the physical properties of the things that have it: not, at any rate, if by "physical property" we mean all and only those properties that might figure in the laws of physics. None of this is mysterious, and none of it is scientifically disreputable.

The advantage of considering this simple case is that it is clear what is going on: The property of being a pawn comes to be attached to certain physically very various objects because there is a particular social practice in which those objects have been taken up, with the result that the rules of this practice can now be applied to all these objects, despite their physical variety. Those rules govern the behavior of chess pieces only in the sense that they tell us which sorts of behavior will count as correct, and which as incorrect. They do not govern the behavior of these chess pieces in the same way that the laws of physics govern the behavior of their constituent atoms. There are no explanatory contexts in which the rules of chess and the laws of physics are in competition.

Having seen how this works quite unproblematically in the case of chess, we can now see that something similar operates in other contexts (and, by doing so, we can approach the idea that it is quite legitimate for psychiatric explanations to make reference to social facts, without thereby being committed to finding any neurological correlates of those facts in the brain, where they might be detected in a brain scanner).

Some features of the chess example are inessential to the point that we are using it to illustrate. The rules of chess are relatively easy to state, and it would be plausible to suppose that they are explicitly represented in the long-term memories of chess players. The rules of other games are less likely to be represented in a psychologically unified way. Soccer is an example. One *might* read a book in which the rules of soccer have been codified, and might even commit these rules to memory, but few people bother to do so. For most purposes, soccer players can rely on a somewhat inchoate grasp of the game's requirements, pieced together from a combination of observations, explicit instruction, and an acquired skill for judging what sort of play seems right. Even when the rules of a game are represented explicitly, there is a limit to what they can tell us. Someone with a knowledge of the rules of chess would be in a strong position, if they knew the physical configuration of a chess board, to deduce the state of play, and perhaps even to make a prediction as to the game's likely outcome. Someone knowing the rules of soccer would find it very much harder to make any such deductions, even if they were given a complete account of the physical configuration of the players and the ball. That is not only because the rules of soccer are more numerous than the rule of chess, and allow room for differences of opinion as to what is and is not permitted. It is also because the factors determining the state of play in a soccer match are distributed over a vastly complex system, which develops through time in a way that defies even the most sophisticated attempts at prediction.

The points that we saw in the case of chess can easily be generalized to the case of soccer, despite these considerable differences between the ways in which the two practices operate.[159] Just as participation in the game of chess can endow a bottle cap with the property of being a pawn, so participation in the game of soccer can endow a person with the property of being a goalkeeper. If you want to know what it is that makes some bottle cap a pawn, it will, we have seen, be a mistake to look at the molecules from which that cap is constituted, or at any of the cap's intrinsic physical properties. The same molecules were present, and the same properties instantiated, even when this bottle cap was not serving as a pawn. Similarly, if you want to know what makes some person a goalkeeper, it will be a mistake to put the person into a scanner, in order to examine the biochemical constituents of their brain, or of their body.

Notice now that, although it would be a mistake to look at physical properties when explaining why some person has the property of being a goalkeeper (just as it would be a mistake to look at physical properties when explaining why some bottle cap has the property of being a pawn), it might *not* be a mistake to look at those physical properties when we are explaining why some person is a *successful* or an *unsuccessful* goalkeeper, or when we are explaining why some bottle cap does good or poor service as a pawn. Perhaps the person's shortcomings in the goal are explained by the length of his arms, or the slowness of his reflexes. Perhaps the bottle cap's shortcomings as a pawn are explained by the stickiness of its surface, or its tendency to be blown away by the wind. The having of short arms is a perfectly explicable physical property, so, too, is the having of slow reflexes, or the having of a sticky surface.

If we wanted to fill in the details of these explanations, we would need to make reference to the interplay between the intrinsic physical properties belonging to these things – such as the shortness of the goalkeeper's arms, or the stickiness of the pawn's surface – and the rules and proceedings of the larger games in which they are participants. To explain how the bottle cap comes to be a rather dysfunctional pawn, we would have to explain both how it comes to be a pawn, and why it functions badly in this role. Doing this would require us to mention the larger game in which it gets taken up, and it would require us to mention the stickiness that impedes its movement on the board. To explain how the sportsman comes to be a rather unsuccessful goalkeeper, we would need to explain both how he comes to be a goalkeeper, and why this role is one that he plays badly. Doing this would involve us mentioning the larger game in which he plays a role, and it would involve mentioning the short arms that impede his reaching to the corners of the goalmouth.

An examination of intrinsic physical properties would have an ineliminable role in these explanations, but it could never make the examination of broader contexts redundant. The two parts of these explanations need to be taken together. It is only when we see them in the context of some practice that short arms show themselves to be a deficit. And it is only in the context of this particular social practice that we can see there to be a single category – the category of goalkeeping deficits – in which short arms and slow reflexes both belong.

Given the points that we have seen in the earlier parts of our discussion, the extrapolation from here to the case of mental disorders should be reasonably straightforward. In Part One of this book we said that, since humans are social animals, social factors contribute to our conception of what it is to be a flourishing human. When we asked what makes a mental disorder disorderly, we found that this social conception of human flourishing has many facets, and is therefore hard to codify. There were some contexts in which that lack of codification left us unable to give principled arguments – we were, for example, unable to find any principled reason for saying that competence in chess has no essential role in one's flourishing as a human – but this somewhat nebulous conception of human flourishing nonetheless seemed to be one that we could operate with, for the purposes of recognizing when it is that significant disruptions to flourishing have occurred.

If living a human life requires that one participate in some social practices, much as being a pawn requires an object to be taken up in a game of chess, then the facts in virtue of which a human flourishes, or fails to flourish, need not be grounded exclusively in that person's intrinsic physical properties, any more than the facts in virtue of which the bottle cap qualifies as a good or bad pawn need to be grounded exclusively in the intrinsic physical properties of that bottle cap. To fully explain the way in which a person's mental life comes to be disorderly, we will need to explain the ways in which they flourish, and the ways in which that flourishing is impeded. This will involve us making some reference to this person's social context, and to the roles that they play within it. It might also require us to make reference to the intrinsic physical features of this person. As they did when we explained the shortcomings of our short-armed goalkeeper, the two parts of this explanation need to work together.

Those parts of the explanation in which we cite a person's physical properties would not make the examination of that person's social contexts redundant, nor vice versa. The relative importance of the social and the neurological will vary from case to case.

There may be some explanatory contexts in which the facts revealed by a brain scan will be the only ones that we need to cite. If the thing that we are hoping to explain is the fact that some particular person bursts into tears at some particular moment, unprovoked by any event in their surroundings, then the occurences going on in that person's brain might have excellent credentials for doing this explanatory work. But the things that psychiatry needs to explain only rarely have this degree of fine-grained particularity. Psychiatrists are typically concerned with much more general tendencies for mental disorderliness, manifesting themselves over much more extended episodes. Rather than predicting whether some person will burst into tears in the next ten seconds, the psychiatrist will typically want to predict whether that person will be vulnerable to sustained sadness over a period of weeks or months, given the manifold social influences that will intervene over that time. The traces left in the brain by these influences might take quite various forms. A list of these neural correlates is likely to be disunified, or arbitrary. Our predictions can be made on a more unified and generalizable basis if they are made directly on the basis of social and psychological facts, rather than being made on the basis of their neurological correlates.[160]

By thinking of mental disorders in this light, we can come to see why it would be a mistake to insist that all such disorders be explained by reference to brain states alone. We can thereby see why the recent attempts to inaugurate a new age of brain-based psychiatry might be built on a misplaced ambition.[161]

There is no telling, in advance, which sorts of facts will be the most useful ones to know about for the purposes of providing psychiatric help. There is no general reason to think that brain facts will, in all cases, have better explanatory credentials than social facts. In most cases of mental disorder, there is evidence suggesting that both sorts of fact are likely to make a contribution.

The earlier parts of this book have examined a number of cases that illustrate this. In order to decide how best to treat the disorderliness that impairs the flourishing of some person with Oppositional defiant disorder, with Autism spectrum disorder, or with a Delusional disorder, we have seen that it will be necessary to understand – and perhaps even to morally evaluate – the social norms that feature in the background against which that person's flourishing needs to be achieved. An examination of the brain cannot make this examination of social contexts redundant. We should not expect the development of brain-scanning techniques to provide us with a shortcut, by which psychiatrists can avoid venturing into cultural and philosophical territories. The practice of psychiatry cannot avoid giving a role to moral, social, and philosophical questions. It must be willing to consider everything.

# Notes to Chapter 3.4

137   Elaine Showalter gives an influential (and controversial) account of the role of cultural forces in the epidemic spread of some mental conditions in her 1997 book *Hystories: Hysterical Epidemics and Modern Culture* (Columbia University Press).

138   For philosophical discussion of these attempts to start afresh in our categorization of mental disorders, see the several papers collected in the 2014 volume, edited by Peter Zachar, Drozdstoj St Stoyanov, Massimiliano Aragona, and Assen Jablensky, *Alternative Perspectives on Psychiatric Validation: DSM, ICD, RDoC, and Beyond* (Oxford University Press).

139   Some of the recent developments in machine learning are discussed, and their promise in applications pertaining to medicine are advertised, in an article by Hayit Greenspan, Bram van Ginneken, and Ronald M. Summers, "Deep learning in medical imaging: Overview and future promise of an exciting new technique." *IEEE Transactions on Medical Imaging* 35, no. 5 (2016): 1153–1159.

140   The National Institute of Mental Health's attempt to put the diagnostic categories of psychiatry onto a new footing is conducted under the rather inperspicuous name of "RDoC," which abbreviates "Research Domain Criteria." A discussion of the rationale for this initiative can be found in an article by Thomas R. Insel and Bruce N. Cuthbert, published in *Science* 348, no. 6234 (2015): 499–500, under the title "Brain disorders? Precisely." John H. Krystal and Matthew W. State review the progress of research that takes this approach in their article, "Psychiatric disorders: Diagnosis to therapy." *Cell* 157, no. 1 (2014): 201–214.

141   The website of the University of Cambridge says, on one of its pages, that:

Pigeon-holing mental illness as "psychiatric" means patients receive inadequate treatment. We want to change that.

The way in which they are trying to change it is, they say, by "treating molecule and mind together." See https://www.philanthropy.cam.ac.uk/give-to-cambridge/mental-health-treating-molecule-and-mind-together

142   Opportunities and challenges for the development of new drug treatments for mental disorders are discussed by Thomas R. Insel in his paper,

"Next-generation treatments for mental disorders." *Science Translational Medicine* 4, no. 155 (2012): 155ps19.

143   David A. Mrazek and Caryn Lerman discuss the potential for innovations in genetics to be used in improving the process of drug prescription in their article, "Facilitating clinical implementation of pharmacogenomics." *JAMA: Journal of the American Medical Association* 306, no. 3 (2011): 304–305.

144   Large claims are often made on behalf of ELIZA, a computer program developed in the 1960s, which imitates a "person centered" psychotherapist. Its creator, Joseph Weizenbaum, suggested that many people were inclined to attribute deep understandings to the program.  It seems unlikely that many 21st-century users would be taken in by the same tricks.  Eliza's repertoire of responses is rather limited, and it isn't long before conversations with it degenerate into nonsense, as the reader can see for themselves by visiting Norbert Landsteiner's implementation of the program at http://www.masswerk.at/elizabot/

Weizenbaum's account of the program can be found in his 1976 book *Computer Power and Human Reason: From Judgment To Calculation* (W.H. Freeman).

145   Adam S. Miner, Arnold Milstein, and Jefferey T. Hancock discuss the prospects for computers taking the role of therapists, in delivering talking cures for mental disorders, in their article "Talking to machines about personal mental health problems." *JAMA: Journal of the American Medical Association* 318, no. 13 (2017): 1217–1218.

146   Kathleen Kara Fitzpatrick, Alison Darcy, and Molly Vierhile present the results of an experiment looking at the efficacy of chatbot-based therapy in "Delivering cognitive behavior therapy to young adults with symptoms of depression and anxiety using a fully automated conversational agent (Woebot): A randomized controlled trial." *JMIR Mental Health* 4, no. 2 (2017): e19.

147   For the idea that the human relationship between patient and therapist is crucial to the efficacy of treatment, see the paper by Daniel J. Martin, John P. Garske, and M. Katherine Davis, "Relation of the therapeutic alliance with outcome and other variables: A meta-analytic review." *Journal of Consulting and Clinical Psychology* 68, no. 3 (2000): 438–450.

148   Although it does not focus on the moment of diagnosis, the DSM does indicate some of the ways in which the symptoms of Histrionic personality disorder introduce complications to the relationship between patients and their therapists, noting that patients may dramatically embellish events, in order to make themselves the cynosure of social and clinical occasions:

This need [viz. to be the centre of attention] is often apparent in their behavior with a clinician (e.g. being flattering, bringing gifts, providing dramatic descriptions of physical and psychological symptoms that are replaced by new symptoms each visit). (*DSM-5*, p. 667)

149   A pessimistic prediction about the abilities of computer chess programs can be found on p. 678 of Douglas R. Hofstadter's 1979 book *Gödel, Escher, Bach: An Eternal Golden Braid* (Basic Books). Garry Kasparov gives his own account of the way in which this prediction was thwarted in his (2017) *Deep Thinking: Where Machine Intelligence Ends and Human Creativity Begins* (Public Affairs). The recent progress in computer Go playing is reported in a paper by David Silver *et al.* "Mastering the game of go without human knowledge." *Nature* 550, no. 7676 (2017): 354-359.

Writing in the same year as Hofstadter, John Haugeland made the case for pessimism about machine translation in his "Understanding natural language." *The Journal of Philosophy* 76, no. 11 (1979): 619–632. The computational systems that achieve better-than-expected translations are discussed by Alon Halevy, Peter Norvig, and Fernando Pereira in their article, "The unreasonable effectiveness of data." *IEEE Intelligent Systems* 24, no 2 (2009): 8–12.

150   An example of computational diagnosis can be found in work that was presented in 2017 by Dong Nie and his collaborators: "Medical image synthesis with context-aware generative adversarial networks." *International Conference on Medical Image Computing and Computer-Assisted Intervention* (Springer), 417–425.

151   The argument that social factors must show up in the brain, in order to be explanatorily relevant to psychology, can be found in a 2012 article by Kirsten Weir, published in the American Psychological Association's *Monitor on Psychology*, under the title "The roots of mental illness: How much of mental illness can the biology of the brain explain?" *Monitor on Psychology* 43, no. 6 (2012): 30–33.

152   For research into the social factors contributing to Schizophrenia, and into the causally relevant traces that these might leave in the brain, see Ceren Akdeniz, Heike Tost, and Andreas Meyer-Lindenberg's paper, "The neurobiology of social environmental risk for schizophrenia: An evolving research field." *Social Psychiatry and Psychiatric Epidemiology* 49, no. 4 (2014): 507–517.

153   The literature cited in footnotes 134–136 is also pertinent here.

154   Newton is shown on p. 131 in a study drawn from the 1689 portrait by Godfrey Kneller.

155   For a useful discussion of the different senses of "reductionism," and of the ways in which Newton's physical explanations were and were not reductive, see Paul M. Churchland and Patricia S. Churchland's paper, "Intertheoretic reduction: A neuroscientists' fieldguide", published as Chapter Five in John Cornwell (ed.) *Nature's Imagination: The Frontiers of Scientific Vision* (Oxford University Press, 1995), 64–77. The most comprehensive discussion of the varieties of reductionism is that given by Carl Gillett in his 2016 book, *Reduction and Emergence in Science and Philosophy* (Cambridge University Press).

156   Although we make the point here by reference to early modern physics, the physics that was developed in the 20th century offers even clearer illustrations of the idea that scientific explanations need not be given by reference to the behaviors of the component parts of the things that are being explained. Roger Penrose discusses this, using examples from topology and quantum physics, in his 1995 paper "Must mathematical physics be reductionist?", which, like the paper by Churchland and Churchland that was cited above, is published in *Nature's Imagination* (pp. 12–26) edited by John Cornwell (Oxford University Press).

157   In taking features of games to illuminate philosophical puzzles about the mind, we are following in a tradition of thinking that was established by Ludwig Wittgenstein, and that is best represented in his *Philosophical Investigations,* a book that was posthumously published in 1953 (Blackwell). Useful discussion of this tactic's general strengths and limitations can be found in Russell Hardin's paper, "Norms and games." *Philosophy of Science* 75, no. 5 (2008): 843–849.

158   Wilfrid Sellars makes his remarks about "Texas chess" in a 1963 paper, "Abstract Entities." *Review of Metaphysics* 16, no 4 (1963): 627–671. Jaroslav Peregrin gives a discussion of the philosophical significance of Sellars' point in his 2007 paper, "Developing Sellars's semantic legacy: Meaning as a role." *Poznan Studies in the Philosophy of the Sciences and the Humanities* 92, no. 1 (2007): 257–274.

159   Although it serves as a useful illustrative example, the game of chess is rather an unusual social practice, in having rules that are so clear, and that have been so unambiguously codified. For some centuries there has been no real room for disagreement as to what the rules of chess are, nor as to whether any particular move is permitted by them, although even here there is some

variation: Castling is not permitted by the rules of chess as it is played in much of Asia.

In other social practices there is very much more fuzziness at the border between that which is permitted by the rules and that which is not. Sometimes this fuzziness arises because there is disagreement as to what the rules are. There are, for example, many different conventions as to how the game of pool should begin. Sometimes the fuzziness arises because the rules of a practice themselves allow some latitude: The referees in soccer matches have more opportunities to exercise judgment than do the stewards of a chess match, for example. In yet other cases it is because there is an intermediate case between that which is ruled out entirely, and that which is penalized within the game. In soccer, for example, the handling of the ball is penalized within the game: the rules explicitly state that, unless the advantage is played, ball-handling results in a free kick or penalty to the opposing team. The rules of soccer make no such explicit proscription of riding on horseback, since that is ruled out of the game in a much more fundamental way. If one of the players handles the ball then the game continues according to the codified rules, with a free kick being awarded. But if one of the players mounts a horse then something other than a game of soccer has now started to take place, and some quite different set of social norms starts to operate. In our attempt to understand rule-governed social practices, we need to operate with more than just the two categories of that which is permitted by the rules, and that which is not.

The fuzzy borderline between that which is permitted and that which is not is, in some practices, very wide indeed. There is, for example, a very large gray area between what is, and what is not, permissible to do with one's knife and fork while at a dinner party. (Readers who think they have a precise conception of this distinction are invited to consider the correct way to proceed when faced with a knife, a fork, and a bunch of bananas.) The existence of this gray area provides unlimited opportunities for disapproving aunties. Manuals that purport to remove the gray area, by providing a codification of these rules, are invariably spurious, since the gray area, and the opportunities for arbitrary disapproval that are created by it, give this particular social practice much of its *raison d'être*.

Philosophical discussion of games and the rules that govern them can be found in Bernard Suits's book *The Grasshopper: Games, Life, and Utopia*, the third edition of which was published in 2014 by Broadview Press. Games are seen from a rather different philosophical perspective in the final sections of Douglas R. Hofstadter's "Analogies and Roles in Human and Machine Thinking," which is reprinted as Chapter 24 in his (1985) *Metamagical Themas: Questing for the Essence of Mind and Pattern* (Basic Books).

160    As we noted when we first met the causal exclusion problem in Part One of this book, a philosophically thorough treatment of the idea that we are gesturing toward can be found in Chapter 8, "Mental causation," and Chapter 10, "Wide causation," in the first volume of Stephen Yablo's philosophical papers: *Thoughts* (Oxford University Press, 2008).

161    For a thorough critique of the various types of reductionism that are at play in psychiatry, and for an elucidation of the role played by social factors, see Laurence J. Kirmayer and Ian Gold's "Re-socializing psychiatry: Critical neuroscience and the limits of reductionism," published as Chapter 15 in the 2015 book, *Critical Neuroscience: A Handbook of the Social and Cultural Contexts of Neuroscience,* edited by Suparna Choudhury and Jan Slaby (Wiley-Blackwell), 307–330.

# Bibliography

Achinstein, Peter. "Function statements." *Philosophy of Science* 44, no. 3 (1977): 341–367.

Agich, George J. "Implications of a pragmatic theory of disease for the DSMs." In *Descriptions and Prescriptions: Values, Mental Disorders, and the DSMs*, by John Z. Sadler, 96–113. Baltimore MD: Johns Hopkins University Press, 2002.

Akagi, Hiroko, and Allan House. "The clinical epidemiology of hysteria: Vanishingly rare, or just vanishing?" *Psychological Medicine* 32, no. 2 (2002): 191–194.

Akdeniz, Ceren, Heike Tost, and Andreas Meyer-Lindenberg. "The neurobiology of social environmental risk for schizophrenia: An evolving research field." *Social Psychiatry and Psychiatric Epidemiology* 49, no. 4 (2014): 507–517.

Alarcón, Renato D. "Culture, cultural factors and psychiatric diagnosis: Review and projections." *World Psychiatry* 8, no. 3 (2009): 131–139.

Al-Issa, Ihsan. "The illusion of reality or the reality of illusion: Hallucinations and culture." *British Journal of Psychiatry* 166, no. 3 (1995): 368–373.

Alter, Torin, and Sven Walter. *Phenomenal Concepts and Phenomenal Knowledge: New Essays on Consciousness and Physicalism*. Oxford: Oxford University Press, 2006.

American Psychiatric Association. *Diagnostic and Statistical Manual of Mental Disorders (5th ed.)*. Washington, DC: American Psychiatric Publishing, 2013.

Amundsen, Ron. "Against normal function." *Studies in History and Philosophy of Science Part C: Studies in History and Philosophy of Biological and Biomedical Sciences* 31, no. 1 (2000): 33–53.

Appiah, Kwame Anthony, and Amy Gutmann. *Color Conscious: The Political Morality of Race*. Princeton, NJ: Princeton University Press, 1998.

Ariew, André, Robert Cummins, and Mark Perlman. *Functions: New Essays in the Philosophy of Psychology and Biology*. New York, NY: Oxford University Press, 2002.

Aristotle. *The Complete Works of Aristotle*. Edited by Jonathan Barnes. Princeton, NJ: Princeton University Press, 1984.

Arpaly, Nomy. "How it is not 'just like diabetes': Mental disorders and the moral psychologist." *Philosophical Issues* 15, no. 1 (2005): 282–298.

Ayers, Michael. *Locke: Epistemology and Ontology.* London: Routledge, 1991.

Ayob, Gloria. "Do people defy generalizations?: Examining the case against evidence-based medicine in psychiatry." *Philosophy, Psychiatry & Psychology* 15, no. 2 (2008): 167–174.

Bagwell, Catherine L., Andrew F. Newcomb, and William M. Bukowski. "Preadolescent friendship and peer rejection as predictors of adult adjustment." *Child Development* 69, no. 1 (1998): 140–153.

Baron-Cohen, Simon. "Is Asperger syndrome necessarily viewed as a disability?" *Focus on Autism and Other Developmental Disabilities* 17, no. 3 (2002): 186–191.

Bayne, Tim, and Michelle Montague. *Cognitive Phenomenology.* Oxford: Oxford University Press, 2011.

Bird, Alexander, and Emma Tobin. "Natural kinds". *The Stanford Encyclopedia of Philosophy.* Edited by Edward N. Zalta. 2018. https://plato.stanford.edu/archives/spr2018/entries/natural-kinds/.

Block, Ned. "Troubles with functionalism." *Minnesota Studies in the Philosophy of Science* 9 (1978): 261–325.

Bock, Carl Ernst. *Atlas of Human Anatomy.* Leipzig: Kraufsu & Eltzner, 1879.

Bolton, Derek. "Classification and causal mechanisms: A deflationary approach to the classification problem." In *Philosophical Issues in Psychiatry II: Nosology,* by Kenneth S. Kendler and Josef Parnas, 6–11. Oxford: Oxford University Press, 2012.

Botha, Derek. "Anorexia nervosa: A fresh perspective." *Theory & Psychology* 25, no. 3 (2015): 328–345.

Bourgery, Jean-Marc, and Nicolas Henri Jacob. *Anatomie de l'homme.* Paris: Guerin, 1862.

Broome, Matthew R. "Taxonomy and ontology in psychiatry: A survey of recent literature." *Philosophy, Psychiatry & Psychology* 13, no. 4 (2006): 303–319.

Buss, David M., and Todd K. Shackelford. "Human aggression in evolutionary psychological perspective." *Clinical Psychology Review* 17, no. 6 (1997): 605–619.

Butler, Judith. *Excitable Speech: A Politics of the Performative.* New York, NY: Routledge, 1997.

Byrne, Peter. "Psychiatric stigma: Past, passing and to come." *Journal of the Royal Society of Medicine* 90, no. 11 (1997): 618–621.

Campbell, Joseph Keim, Michael O'Rourke, and Matthew H. Slater. *Carving Nature at its Joints: Natural kinds in metaphysics and science.* Cambridge, MA: MIT Press, 2011.

Campbell, Kenneth. "A case of hysterical amblyopia." *British Medical Journal* 2, no. 2855 (1915): 434.

Carbone, Eric. "Arranging the classroom with an eye (and ear) to students with ADHD." *Teaching Exceptional Children* 34, no. 2 (2001): 72–82.

Carroll, John W. *Laws of Nature.* Cambridge: Cambridge University Press, 1994.

Chalmers, David J. "Facing up to the problem of consciousness." *Journal of Consciousness Studies* 2, no. 3 (1995): 200–219.

—. *The Conscious Mind: In Search of a Fundamental Theory.* Oxford: Oxford University Press, 1996.

Churchland, Paul M., and Patricia S. Churchland. "Intertheoretic reduction: A neuroscientists' fieldguide." In *Nature's Imagination: The Frontiers of Scientific Vision,* edited by John Cornwell, 64–77. Oxford: Oxford University Press, 1995.

Clare, Anthony. *Psychiatry in Dissent: Controversial Issues in Thought and Practice.* 2nd Edition. London: Tavistock Publications, 1980.

Claridge, Gordon. *Origins of Mental Illness: Temperament, Deviance and Disorder.* Oxford: Basil Blackwell, 1985.

Cohen, Jonathan, and Craig Callender. "Special sciences, conspiracy and the better best system account of lawhood." *Erkenntnis* 73, no. 3 (2010): 427–447.

Conelea, Christine A., and Douglas W. Woods. "The influence of contextual factors on tic expression in Tourette's syndrome: A review." *Journal of Psychosomatic Research* 65, no. 5 (2008): 487–496.

Conrad, Peter. *The Medicalization of Society: On the Transformation of Human Conditions into Treatable Disorders.* Baltimore, MD: Johns Hopkins University Press, 2008.

Conrad, Peter, and Joseph W. Schneider. *Deviance and Medicalization: From Badness to Sickness.* St. Louis: The C.V. Mosby Company, 1980.

Craddock, Nick, and Michael J. Owen. "The beginning of the end for the Kraepelinian dichotomy." *British Journal of Psychiatry* 186, no. 5 (2005): 364–366.

Craver, Carl F. *Explaining the Brain: Mechanisms and the Mosaic Unity of Neuroscience.* Oxford: Oxford University Press, 2009.

Darwin, Charles. *The Origin of Species by Means of Natural Selection.* Edited by J.W. Burrow. London: Penguin Books, 1859/1985.

Davies, Gayle. "Health and sexuality." In *The Oxford Handbook of the History of Medicine,* by Mark Jackson, 503–523. Oxford: Oxford University Press, 2011.

Dennett, Daniel C. *Brainchildren: Essays on Designing Minds.* Cambridge, MA: MIT Press, 1998.

—. *Consciousness Explained.* London: Penguin Books, 1991.

—. *Elbow Room: The Varieties of Free Will Worth Wanting.* Cambridge, MA: MIT Press, 1984.

—. "Instead of qualia." In *Consciousness in Philosophy and Cognitive Neuroscience*, edited by Antti Revonsuo and Matti Kamppinen, 129–139. Hillsdale, NJ: Lawrence Erlbaum, 1994.

Dolnick, Edward. *Madness on the Couch: Blaming the Victim in the Heyday of Psychoanalysis.* New York, NY: Simon and Schuster, 1998.

Doris, Eli, Ia Shekriladze, Nino Javakhishvili, Roshan Jones, Janet Treasure, and Kate Tchanturia. "Is cultural change associated with eating disorders? A systematic review of the literature." *Eating and Weight Disorders: Studies on Anorexia, Bulimia and Obesity* 20, no. 2 (2015): 149–160.

Douglas, Ron, and Mustafa Djamgoz. *The Visual System of Fish.* London: Chapman and Hall, 1990.

Durkheim, Émile. *Le suicide: étude de sociologie.* Paris: F. Alcan, 1897.

—. *Suicide: A Study in Sociology.* Edited by George Simpson. Translated by John A. Spaulding and George Simpson. Glencoe, IL: Free Press, 1951.

Emmerton, Jacky, and Juan D. Delhis. "Wavelength discrimination in the 'visible' and ultraviolet spectrum by pigeons." *Journal of Comparative Physiology* 141, no. 1 (1980): 47–52.

Engel, George L. "The clinical application of the biopsychosocial model." *American Journal of Psychiatry* 137, no. 5 (1980): 535–544.

Evans, Gary W. "The built environment and mental health." *Journal of Urban Health* 80, no. 4 (2003): 536–555.

Fanon, Frantz. *Black Skin, White Masks.* Translated by Charles Lam Markmann. London: Pluto Press, 2017.

—. *Les damnés de la terre.* Paris: F. Maspero, 1961.

—. *Peau noire, masques blancs.* Paris: Editions du Seuil, 1952.

—. *The Wretched of the Earth.* Translated by Richard Philcox. New York, NY: Grove Press, 2004.

Faucher, Luc. "Darwinian blues: Evolutionary psychiatry and depression." In *Sadness or Depression?: International Perspectives on the Depression Epidemic and Its Meaning*, edited by Jerome C. Wakefield and Steeves Demazeux, 69–94. Dordrecht: Springer, 2016.

Feigl, Herbert. "The 'mental' and the 'physical'." *Minnesota Studies in the Philosophy of Science* 2 (1958): 370–497.

—. *The "Mental" and the "Physical": The Essay and a Postscript.* Minneapolis, MN: University of Minnesota Press, 1967.

Fenton, Andrew, and Tim Krahn. "Autism, neurodiversity, and equality beyond the 'normal'." *Journal of Ethics in Mental Health* 2, no. 2 (2007): 1–6.

Fergusson, David M., Nicola R. Swain-Campbell, and L. John Horwood. "Deviant peer affiliations, crime and substance use: A fixed effects regression analysis." *Journal of Abnormal Child Psychology* 30, no. 4 (2002): 419–430.

Figuier, Louis. *Les merveilles de la science, ou description populaire des inventions modernes.* Paris: Furne, Jouvet et Cie, 1867.

Fischer, John Martin, Robert Kane, Derk Pereboom, and Manuel Vargas. *Four Views on Free Will.* Oxford: Blackwell Publishing, 2007.

Fitzpatrick, Kathleen Kara, Alison Darcy, and Molly Vierhile. "Delivering cognitive behavior therapy to young adults with symptoms of depression and anxiety using a fully automated conversational agent (Woebot): A randomized controlled trial." *Journal of Medical Internet Research: Mental Health* 4, no. 2 (2017): e19.

Foot, Philippa. *Natural Goodness.* Oxford: Clarendon Press, 2001.

Foucault, Michel. *Folie et déraison: histoire de la folie à l'âge classique.* Paris: Union Générale d'Éditions, 1961.

—. *Histoire de la sexualité .* 4 vols. Paris: Gallimard, 1976–2018.

—. *Madness and Civilization: A History of Insanity in the Age of Reason.* Translated by Richard Howard. London: Routledge, 1989.

—. *Naissance de la clinique: une archéologie du regard médical.* Paris: Presses universitaires de France, 1963.

—. *The Birth of the Clinic.* Translated by A.M. Sheridan Smith. New York, NY: Pantheon Books, 1973.

Freud, Sigmund. *Totem And Taboo: The Complete Psychological Works of Sigmund Freud Vol. 13.* Edited by James Strachey. New York, NY: Vintage Classics, 1950/2001.

—. *Totem und Tabu: Einige Übereinstimmungen im Seelenleben der Wilden und der Neurotiker.* Leipzig: Internationaler Psychoanalytischer Verlag, 1922.

Frye, Marilyn. *The Politics of Reality: Essays in Feminist Theory.* Trumansburg, NY: Crossing Press, 1983.

Gerrans, Philip. "Mechanisms of madness: Evolutionary psychiatry without evolutionary psychology." *Biology and Philosophy* 22, no. 1 (2007): 35–56.

Gert, Bernard, and Charles M. Culver. "Defining mental disorder." In *The Philosophy of Psychiatry: A Companion*, edited by Jennifer Radden, 415–425. Oxford: Oxford University Press, 2004.

Ghaerni, S. Nassir. "Taking disease seriously: Beyond 'pragmatic' nosology." In *Philosophical Issues in Psychiatry II: Nosology*, edited by Kenneth S. Kendler and Josef Parnas, 42–72. Oxford: Oxford University Press, 2012.

Gibb, Sophie C., Rögnvaldur Ingthorsson, and E. Jonathan Lowe. *Mental Causation and Ontology.* Oxford: Oxford University Press, 2013.

Gillett, Carl. *Reduction and Emergence in Science and Philosophy.* Cambridge: Cambridge University Press, 2016.

Glackin, Shane N. "Tolerance and illness: The politics of medical and psychiatric classification." *Journal of Medicine and Philosophy* 35, no. 4 (2010): 449–465.

Goetzman, William N., Dasol Kim, Alok Kumar, and Qin Wang. "Weather-induced mood, institutional investors, and stock returns." *The Review of Financial Studies* 28, no. 1 (2015): 73–111.

Gold, Joel, and Ian Gold. "The 'Truman Show' delusion: Psychosis in the global village." *Cognitive Neuropsychiatry* 17, no. 6 (2012): 455–472.

Graham, George. *The Disordered Mind: An Introduction to Philosophy of Mind and Mental Illness*. 2nd Edition. Abingdon: Routledge, 2013.

Graham, Linda J. "From ABCs to ADHD: The role of schooling in the construction of behaviour disorder and production of disorderly objects." *International Journal of Inclusive Education* 12, no. 1 (2008): 7–33.

Greenspan, Hayit, Bram van Ginneken, and Ronald M. Summers. "Deep learning in medical imaging: Overview and future promise of an exciting new technique." *IEEE Transactions on Medical Imaging* 35, no. 5 (2016): 1153–1159.

Guze, S.B. *Why Psychiatry is a Branch of Medicine*. New York, NY: Oxford University Press, 1992.

Hacking, Ian. *Historical Ontology*. Cambridge, MA: Harvard University Press, 2002.

—. "Making up people." In *Reconstructing Individualism: Autonomy, Individuality, and the Self in Western Thought*, edited by Thomas Heller, Morton Sosna and David E. Wellbery, 222–236. Stanford, CA: Stanford University Press, 1986.

—. *Rewriting the Soul: Multiple Personality and the Sciences of Memory*. Princeton, NJ: Princeton University Press, 1995.

—. "The looping effects of human kinds." In *Causal Cognition: A Multidisciplinary Debate*, edited by Dan Sperber, David Premack and Ann J. Premack, 351–394. Oxford: Clarendon Press, 1995.

Halevy, Alon, Peter Norvig, and Fernando Pereira. "The unreasonable effectiveness of data." *IEEE Intelligent Systems* 24, no. 2 (2009): 8–12.

Hardin, Russell. "Norms and games." *Philosophy of Science* 75, no. 5 (2008): 843–849.

Harman, Gilbert. "The inference to the best explanation." *Philosophical Review* 74, no. 1 (1965): 88–95.

Haugeland, J. "Understanding natural language." *The Journal of Philosophy* 76, no. 11 (1979): 619–632.

Hawkins, J. David, Richard F. Catalano, and Janet Y. Miller. "Risk and protective factors for alcohol and other drug problems in adolescence and early adulthood: Implications for substance abuse prevention." *Psychological Bulletin* 112, no. 1 (1992): 64–105.

Hempel, Carl G., and Paul Oppenheim. "Studies in the logic of explanation." *Philosophy of Science* 15, no. 2 (1948): 135–175.

Henningsen, Peter, Thorsten Jakobsen, Marcus Schiltenwolf, and Mitchell G. Weiss. "Somatization revisited: Diagnosis and perceived causes of common mental disorders." *The Journal of Nervous and Mental Disease* 193, no. 2 (2005): 85–92.

Hofstadter, Douglas R. *Gödel, Escher, Bach: An Eternal Golden Braid.* New York, NY: Basic Books, 1979.

—. "Analogies and roles in human and machine thinking" Chapter 24 of his *Metamagical Themas: Questing for the Essence of Mind and Pattern.* New York, NY: Basic Books, 1985.

Holmes, Jeremy. "Narrative in psychiatry and psychotherapy: the evidence?" *Medical Humanities* 26, no. 2 (2000): 92–96.

Horgan, Terence E. "From supervenience to superdupervenience: Meeting the demands of a material world." *Mind* 102, no. 408 (1993): 555–586.

Horsfall, Laura J., Irwin Nazareth, Stephen P. Pereira, and Irene Petersen. "Gilbert's syndrome and the risk of death: A population-based cohort study." *Journal of Gastroenterology and Hepatology* 28, no. 10 (2013): 1643–1647.

Horwitz, Allan V., and Jerome C. Wakefield. *The Loss of Sadness: How Psychiatry Transformed Normal Sorrow into Depressive Disorder.* Oxford: Oxford University Press, 2007.

Hu, Yuanreng, and Noreen Goldman. "Mortality differentials by marital status: An international comparison." *Demography* 27, no. 2 (1990): 233–250.

Hume, David. *An Enquiry Concerning Human Understanding.* Edited by L. A. Selby-Bigge. Oxford: Clarendon Press, 1777/1975.

Hursthouse, Rosalind. *On Virtue Ethics.* Oxford: Oxford University Press, 1999.

Insel, Thomas R. "Next-generation treatments for mental disorders." *Science Translational Medicine* 4, no. 155 (2012): 155ps19.

Insel, Thomas R., and Bruce N. Cuthbert. "Brain disorders? Precisely." *Science* 348, no. 6234 (2015): 499–500.

Jackson, Frank. "Epiphenomenal qualia." *Philosophical Quarterly* 32, no. 127 (1982): 127–136.

Jackson, Frank. "What Mary didn't know." *The Journal of Philosophy* 83, no. 5 (1986): 291–295.

Jefferson, Anneli. "What does it take to be a brain disorder?" *Synthese*, April 2018: 1–14.

Kasof, Joseph. "Cultural variation in seasonal depression: Cross-national differences in winter versus summer patterns of seasonal affective disorder." *Journal of Affective Disorders* 115, no. 1 (2009): 79–86.

Kasparov, Garry K. *Deep Thinking: Where Machine Intelligence Ends and Human Creativity Begins.* New York, NY: Public Affairs, 2017.

Kemp, Simon, and Kevin Williams. "Demonic possession and mental disorder in medieval and early modern Europe." *Psychological Medicine* 17, no. 1 (1987): 21–29.

Kendell, Robert E. "The major functional psychoses: Are they independent entities or part of a continuum? Philosophical and conceptual issues underlying the debate." In *Concepts of Mental Disorder: A Continuing Debate*, edited by Alan Kerr and Hamish McClelland, 1–16. London: Gaskell, 1991.

Kendler, Kenneth S. "The nature of psychiatric disorders." *World Psychiatry* 15, no. 1 (2016): 5–12.

Kendler, Kenneth S., Peter Zachar, and Carl Craver. "What kinds of things are psychiatric disorders?" *Psychological Medicine* 41, no. 6 (2011): 1143–1150.

Kim, Jaegwon. *Mind in a Physical World: An Essay on the Mind-Body Problem and Mental Causation.* Cambridge, MA: MIT Press, 1998.

Kirmayer, Laurence J., and Ian Gold. "Re-socializing psychiatry: Critical neuroscience and the limits of reductionism." In *Critical Neuroscience: A Handbook of the Social and Cultural Contexts of Neuroscience*, edited by Suparna Choudhury and Jan Slaby, 307–330. Chichester: Wiley Blackwell, 2012.

Kirmayer, Laurence J., and Norman Sartorius. "Cultural models and somatic syndromes." *Psychosomatic Medicine.* 69, no. 9 (2007): 832-840.

Klerman, Gerald L. "Mental illness, the medical model, and psychiatry." *The Journal of Medicine and Philosophy* 2, no. 3 (1977): 220–243.

Kripke, Saul A. *Naming and Necessity.* Cambridge, MA: Harvard University Press, 1980.

Krystal, John H., and Matthew W. State. "Psychiatric disorders: Diagnosis to therapy." *Cell* 157, no. 1 (2014): 201–214.

Laing, R.D. *The Politics of Experience and The Bird of Paradise.* London: Penguin Books, 1967.

Lange, Marc. "The end of diseases." *Philosophical Topics* 35, no. 1/2 (2007): 265–292.

Lewis, C.I. *Mind and the World Order: Outline of a Theory of Knowledge.* New York, NY: Charles Scribner and Sons, 1929.

Lieberman, Melissa, Lise Gauvin, William M. Bukowski, and White, Donna R. "Interpersonal influence and disordered eating behaviors in adolescent girls: The role of peer modeling, social reinforcement, and body-related teasing." *Eating Behaviors* 2, no. 3 (2001): 215–236.

Link, Bruce G., and Joe Phelan. "Social conditions as fundamental causes of disease." *Journal of Health and Social Behavior* 35, Extra Issue (1995): 80–94.

Lipton, Peter. *Inference to the Best Explanation.* London: Routledge, 1991.

Littlewood, Roland, and Maurice Lipsedge. "The butterfly and the serpent: Culture, psychopathology and biomedicine." *Culture, Medicine and Psychiatry* 11, no. 3 (1987): 289–335.

Lloyd, Elisabeth A., and Marcus Feldman. "Evolutionary psychology: A view from evolutionary biology." *Psychological Inquiry* 13, no. 2 (2002): 150–156.

Locke, John. *An Essay Concerning Human Understanding*. Amherst, NY: Prometheus Books, 1693/1995.

Lopez-Ibor, Juan J., and Maria-Ines Lopez-Ibor. "Paving the way for new research strategies in mental disorders. First part: The recurring crisis of psychiatry." *Actas Española de Psiquiatría* 41, no. 1 (2013): 33–43.

Luhn, Alec. "Russian protester's sentence of indefinite psychiatric treatment upheld." *The Guardian*, 26 March 2014.

Lukes, Steven. "Methodological individualism reconsidered." *The British Journal of Sociology* 19, no. 2 (1968): 119–129.

Mackie, John L. *Problems from Locke*. Oxford: Oxford University Press, 1976.

Madduz, James E. "Stopping the 'madness': Positive psychology and the deconstruction of the illness ideology and the DSM." In *Handbook of Positive Psychology*, edited by C.R. Snyder and Shane J. Lopez, 13–25. Oxford: Oxford University Press, 2001.

Martin, Daniel J., John P. Garske, and M. Katherine Davis. "Relation of the therapeutic alliance with outcome and other variables: A meta-analytic review." *Journal of Consulting and Clinical Psychology* 68, no. 3 (2000): 438–450.

Martins, Megan P., Sandra L. Harris, and Jan S. Handleman. "Supporting inclusive education." In *Handbook of Autism and Pervasive Developmental Disorders (Vol 2.) Assessment, Interventions, and Policy*, edited by Fred R Volkmar, Sally J. Rogers, Rhea Paul and Kevin A. Pelphrey, 858–870. Hoboken, NJ: John Wiley & Sons, 2014.

Masserman, Jules H., and Hugh T. Carmichael. "Diagnosis and prognosis in psychiatry: With a follow-up study of the results of short-term general hospital therapy of psychiatric cases." *Journal of Mental Science* 84, no. 353 (1938): 893–946.

Maudlin, Tim. "Computation and consciousness." *The Journal of Philosophy* 86, no. 8 (1989): 407–432.

McCulloch, Warren, and Walter Pitts. "A logical calculus of the ideas immanent in nervous activity." *Bulletin of Mathematical Biophysics* 7 (1943): 113–133.

McGhee, George. *Convergent Evolution: Limited Forms Most Beautiful*. Cambridge, MA: MIT Press, 2011.

Meehl, P. E., and A. Rosen. "Antecedent probability and the efficiency of psychometric signs, patterns, or cutting scores." *Psychological Bulletin* 52, no. 3 (1955): 194–216.

Megone, Christopher. "Mental illness, human function, and values." *Philosophy, Psychiatry & Psychology* 7, no. 1 (2000): 45–65.

Meixel, Antonie, Elena Yanchar, and Adriane Fugh-Berman. "Hypoactive sexual desire disorder: Inventing a disease to sell low libido." *Journal of Medical Ethics* 41, no. 10 (2015): 859–862.

Miller, Joshua D., W. Keith Campbell, and Paul A. Pilkonis. "Narcissistic personality disorder: Relations with distress and functional impairment." *Comprehensive Psychiatry* 48, no. 2 (2007): 170–177.

Millikan, Ruth. "Historical kinds and the 'special sciences'." *Philosophical Studies* 95, no. 1–2 (1999): 45–65.

Miner, Adam S., Arnold Milstein, and Jefferey T. Hancock. "Talking to machines about personal mental health problems." *JAMA: The Journal of the American Medical Association* 318, no. 13 (2017): 1217–1218.

Mole, Christopher. "Autism and 'disease': The semantics of an ill-posed question." *Philosophical Psychology* 30, no. 8 (2017): 1126–1140.

Molière. *Le malade imaginaire.* Translated by Henry Thomas Barnwell. London: Grant & Cutler, 1982.

Morris, Jonathan. "Why espresso? Explaining changes in European coffee preferences from a production of culture perspective." *European Review of History: Revue européenne d'histoire* 20, no. 5 (2013): 881–901.

Morrison, Michael A. "Paul Robeson's Othello at the Savoy Theatre 1930." *New Theatre Quarterly* 27, no. 2 (2011): 114–140.

Moser, Charles. "Paraphilia: A critique of a confused concept." In *New Directions in Sex Therapy: Innovations and Alternatives*, edited by Peggy J. Kleinplatz, 91–108. Philadelphia, PA: Taylor and Francis, 2001.

Mrazek, David A., and Caryn Lerman. "Facilitating clinical implementation of pharmacogenomics." *JAMA: Journal of the American Medical Association* 306, no. 3 (2011): 304–305.

Nagel, Thomas. "What is it like to be a bat?" *The Philosophical Review* 83, no. 4 (1974): 435–450.

Nie, Dong, et al. "Medical image synthesis with context-aware generative adversarial networks." *International Conference on Medical Image Computing and Computer-Assisted Intervention.* Cham: Springer, 2017. 417–425.

Norberg, Ulla M. *Vertebrate Flight: Mechanics, Physiology, Morphology, Ecology and Evolution.* Heidelberg: Springer-Verlag, 1990.

Nordby, Knut. "What is this thing you call color: Can a totally color-blind person know about color?" In *Phenomenal Concepts and Phenomenal Knowledge: New Essays on Consciousness and Physicalism*, edited by Torin Alter and Sven Walter, 77–86. Oxford: Oxford University Press, 2007.

O'Riordan, Michelle A., Kate C. Plaisted, Jon Driver, and Simon Baron-Cohen. "Superior visual search in autism." *Journal of Experimental Psychology: Human Perception and Performance* 27, no. 3 (2001): 719–730.

Owen, Jesse, and Frank D. Fincham. "Effects of gender and psychosocial factors on 'friends with benefits' relationships among young adults." *Archives of Sexual Behavior* 40, no. 2 (2011): 311–320.

Papineau, David. "Mental disorder, illness and biological disfunction." *Royal Institute of Philosophy Supplements* 37 (1994): 73–82.

Patrick, Heather, and Theresa A. Nicklas. "A review of family and social determinants of children's eating patterns and diet quality." *Journal of the American College of Nutrition* 24, no. 2 (2005): 83–92.

Pendergraft, Garrett. "In defense of a causal requirement on explanation." In *Causality in the Sciences*, edited by Phyllis McKay Illari, Federica Russo, and Jon Williamson, 470–493. Oxford: Oxford University Press, 2011.

Penrose, Roger. "Must mathematical physics be reductionist?" In *Nature's Imagination: The Frontiers of Scientific Vision*, edited by John Cornwell, 12–26. Oxford: Oxford University Press, 1995.

Peregrin, Jaroslav. "Developing Sellars's semantic legacy: Meaning as a role." *Poznan Studies in the Philosophy of the Sciences and the Humanities* 92, no. 1 (2007): 257–274.

Piper, August, and Harold Merskey. "The Persistence of Folly: A Critical Examination of Dissociative Identity Disorder. Part I. The Excesses of an Improbable Concept." *The Canadian Journal of Psychiatry* 49, no. 9 (2004): 592–600.

Place, Ullin T. "Is consciousness a brain process?" *British Journal of Psychology* 47, no. 1 (1956): 44–50.

Popper, Karl. *Logik der Forschung: Zur Erkenntnistheorie der Modernen Naturwissenschaft*. Vienna: Springer, 1935.

—. *The Logic of Scientific Discovery.* London: Hutchinson & Co., 1959.

—. *The Open Society and Its Enemies.* London: Routledge, 1945.

Price, Huw, and Richard Corry. *Causation, Physics, and the Constitution of Reality: Russell's Republic Revisited.* Oxford: Oxford University Press, 2006.

Putnam, Hilary. "The mental life of some machines." In *Intentionality, Minds and Perception*, edited by Hector-Neri Castañeda, 177–200. Detroit, MI: Wayne State University Press, 1967

Radden, Jennifer. "Epidemic depression and Burtonian melancholy." *Philosophical Papers* 36, no. 3 (2007): 443–464.

—. *Moody Minds Distempered: Essays on Melancholy and Depression.* New York: Oxford University Press, 2009.

Rawls, John. *A Theory of Justice.* Cambridge, MA: Harvard University Press, 1971.

Reinders, A. A. T. Simone, Antoon T. M. Willemsen, Herry P. J. Vos, Johan A. den Boer, and Ellert R. S. Nijenhuis. "Fact or factitious? A psychobiological study of authentic and simulated dissociative identity states." *PLoS One* 7, no. 6 (2012): e39279.

Repetti, Rena L., Shelley E. Taylor, and Teresa E. Seeman. "Risky families: Family social environments and the mental and physical health of offspring." *Psychological Bulletin* 128, no. 2 (2002): 330–366.

Rey, Georges. "A narrow representationalist account of qualitative experience." *Philosophical Perspectives* 12 (1998): 435–458.

Rhoades, Galena K., Claire M. Kamp Dush, David C. Atkins, Scott M. Stanley, and Howard J. Markman. "Breaking up is hard to do: The impact of unmarried relationship dissolution on mental health and life satisfaction." *Journal of Family Psychology* 25, no. 3 (2011): 366–374.

Riddick, Barbara. *Living with Dyslexia: The Social and Emotional Consequences of Specific Learning Difficulties/Disabilities.* London: Routledge, 1996..

Rüsch, Nicolas, Sara Evans-Lacko, and Graham Thornicroft. "What is a mental illness? Public views and their effects on attitudes and disclosure." *Australian & New Zealand Journal of Psychiatry* 46, no. 7 (2012): 641–650.

Sadler, John Z. *Values and Psychiatric Diagnosis.* Oxford: Oxford University Press, 2005.

Samson, Colin. "The fracturing of medical dominance in British psychiatry?" *Sociology of Health & Illness* 17, no. 2 (1995): 245–268.

Sartre, Jean-Paul. *Being and Nothingness: A Phenomenological Essay on Ontology.* Translated by Hazel E. Barnes. New York, NY: Washington Square Press, 1956.

—. *L'être et le néant: Essai d'ontologie phénoménologique.* Paris: Gallimard, 1943.

Satow, Roberta. "Where has all the hysteria gone?" *Psychoanalytic Review* 66, no. 4 (1979): 463–477.

Scerri, Eric R. *The Periodic Table: A Very Short Introduction.* Oxford: Oxford University Press, 2011.

Scheff, Thomas J. "The labelling theory of mental illness." *American Sociological Review* 39, no. 30 (1974): 444–452.

Schomerus, Georg, and Matthias C. Angermeyer. "Stigma and its impact on help-seeking for mental disorders: What do we know?" *Epidemiology and Psychiatric Sciences* 17, no. 1 (2008): 31–37.

Scull, Andrew. *Madness in Civilization: A Cultural History of Insanity.* Princeton, NJ: Princeton University Press, 2015.

—. "Nosologies." *TLS: The Times Literary Supplement,* 18 May 2012.

Searle, John. "Is the brain's mind a computer program?" *Scientific American* 262, no. 1 (1990): 25–31.

Sedikides, Constantine, Eric A. Rudich, Aiden P. Gregg, Madoka Kumashiro, and Caryl Rusbult. "Are normal narcissists psychologically healthy?: Self-esteem matters." *Journal of Personality and Social Psychology* 87, no. 3 (2004): 400–416.

Segal, Judy Z. "Sex, drugs, and rhetoric: The case of flibanserin for 'female sexual dysfunction'." *Social Studies of Science* 48, no. 4 (2018): 459–482.

Sellars, Wilfred. "Abstract entities." *Review of Metaphysics* 16, no. 4 (1963): 627–671.

Seton, Frances. "Opening myself to change." In *Spare Rib Reader*, edited by Marsha Rowe, 410–416. Harmondsworth: Penguin Books, 1982.

Shannon, Claude. "A mathematical theory of communication." *Bell System Technical Journal* 27 (1948): 379–423.

Showalter, Elaine. *Hystories: Hysterical Epidemics and Modern Culture.* New York, NY: Columbia University Press, 1997.

Silver, David, Julian Schrittwieser, Karen Simonyan, Ioannis Antonoglou, Aja Huang, Arthur Guez, Thomas Hubert *et al.* "Mastering the game of go without human knowledge." *Nature* 550, no. 7676 (2017): 354–359.

Simon, Robin W. "Revisiting the relationships among gender, marital status, and mental health." *American Journal of Sociology* 107, no. 4 (2002): 1065–1096

Singer, Charles. *A Short History of Anatomy and Physiology from the Greeks to Harvey.* New York, NY: Dover Books, 1957.

Small, Meredith F. *The Culture of Our Discontent: Beyond the Medical Model of Mental Illness.* Washington, DC: National Academies Press, 2006.

Smart, Jack J.C. "Sensations and brain processes." *Philosophical Review* 68, no. 2 (April 1959): 141–156.

Sobel, Alan G. "Desire: Paraphilia and distress in DSM-IV." In *The Philosophy of Psychiatry: A Companion*, edited by Jennifer Radden, 54–63. Oxford: Oxford University Press, 2004.

Spitzer, Robert L., and Jerome C. Wakefield. "DSM-IV diagnostic criterion for clinical significance: Does it help solve the false positives problem?" *American Journal of Psychiatry* 156, no. 12 (1999): 1856–1864.

Srinivasan, Amia. "The aptness of anger." *Journal of Political Philosophy* 26, no. 2 (2018): 123–144.

Stegenga, Jacob. *Medical Nihilism.* Oxford: Oxford University Press, 2018.

Stein, D.J., K.A. Phillips, D. Bolton, K.W.M. Fulford, J.Z. Sadler, and K.S. Kendler. "What is a mental/psychiatric disorder? From DSM-IV to DSM-V." *Psychological Medicine* 40, no. 11 (2010): 1759–1765.

Stevenson, Michael R. "Public policy, mental health, and lesbian, gay, bisexual and transgender clients." In *Handbook of Counseling and Psychotherapy with Lesbian, Gay, Bisexual, and Transgender Clients*, edited by Kathleen J. Bieschke, Ruperto M. Perez, and Kurt A. DeBord, 379–397. Washington, DC: American Psychological Association, 2007.

Stratton, George Malcolm. *Theophrastus and the Greek Physiological Psychology before Aristotle.* London: G. Allen and Unwin, 1917.

Suits, Bernard. *The Grasshopper: Games, Life, and Utopia.* 3rd Edition. London: Broadview Press, 2014.

Szasz, Thomas S. *The Myth of Mental Illness: Foundations of a Theory of Personal Conduct.* New York, NY: Harper & Row, 1961.

Tekin, Şerife. "Psychiatric taxonomy: At the crossroads of science and ethics." *Journal of Medical Ethics* 40, no. 8 (2014): 513–514.

Tekin, Şerife, and Melissa Mosko. "Hyponarrativity and context-specific limitations of the DSM-5." *Public Affairs Quarterly* 29, no. 1 (2015): 111–136.

Temkin, Owsei. *The Falling Sickness: A History of Epilepsy for the Greeks to the Beginnings of Modern Neurology.* Baltimore, MD: Johns Hopkins University Press, 1945.

The Brainstorm Consortium. "Analysis of shared heritability in common disorders of the brain." *Science* 360, no. 6395 (2018): eaap8757.

*The Economist.* "China wakes up to its mental health problems." 28 January 2017.

Thomas, Philip, Patrick Bracken, and Salma Yasmeen. "Explanatory models for mental illness: Limitations and dangers in a global context." *Pakistan Journal of Neurological Sciences* 2, no. 3 (2007): 176–181.

Thomas, Philip, Patrick Bracken, and Sami Timimi. "The limits of evidence-based medicine in psychiatry." *Philosophy, Psychiatry & Psychology* 19, no. 4 (2012): 295–308.

Thompson, Chrissy, and Mark A. Wood. "A media archaeology of the creepshot." *Feminist Media Studies* 18, no. 4 (2018): 1–15.

Thornton, Tim. "Mental illness and reductionism: Can functions be naturalized?" *Philosophy, Psychiatry & Psychology* 7, no. 1 (2000): 67–76.

Turing, Alan M. "Computing machinery and intelligence." *Mind* 59, no. 236 (1950): 433–460.

—. "On computable numbers, with an application to the Entscheidungsproblem." *Proceedings of the London Mathematical Society* 2, no. 42 (1936): 230–265.

van Inwagen, Peter. *An Essay on Free Will.* Oxford: Oxford University Press, 1983.

Vitebsky, Piers. *The Shaman: Voyages of the Soul, Trance, Ecstasy and Healing From Siberia to the Amazon.* London: Duncan Baird, 1995.

von Neumann, John. *The Computer and the Brain.* New Haven, CT: Yale University Press, 1958.

Wakefield, Jerome C. "Evolutionary versus prototype analysis of the concept of disorder." *Journal of Abnormal Psychology* 108, no. 3 (1999): 374–399.

—. "The concept of mental disorder: On the boundary between biological facts and social values." *American Psychologist* 47, no. 3 (1992): 373–388.

Weir, Kirsten. "The roots of mental illness: How much of mental illness can the biology of the brain explain?" *Monitor on Psychology* 43, no. 6 (2012): 30–33.

Weizenbaum, Joseph. *Computer Power and Human Reason: From Judgment to Calculation.* San Francisco, CA: W.H. Freeman, 1976.

Wittgenstein, Ludwig. *Philosophical Investigations.* Translated by G.E.M. Anscombe. Oxford: Basil Blackwell, 1953.

Woodward, James. *Making Things Happen: A Theory of Causal Explanation.* Oxford: Oxford University Press, 2005.

—. "Mental causation and neural mechanisms." In *Being Reduced: New Essays on Reduction, Explanation, and Causation*, edited by Jakob Hohwy and Jesper Kallestrup, 218–262. Oxford: Oxford University Press, 2008.

World Health Organization. *ICD-10: International Statistical Classification of Diseases and Related Health Problems.* Tenth Revision. Geneva: World Health Organization, 2004.

Wright, David. "'Childlike in his innocence': Lay attitudes to 'idiots' and 'imbeciles' in Victorian England." In *From Idiocy to Mental Deficiency: Historical Perspectives on People with Learning Disabilities*, edited by Anne Digby and David Wright, 118–133. London: Routledge, 1996.

Yablo, Stephen. "Causal relevance." *Philosophical Issues* 13, no. 1 (2003): 316–328.

—. "Mental causation." *Philosophical Review* 101, no. 2 (1992): 245–280.

—. *Thoughts: Philosophical Papers Vol. 1.* Oxford: Oxford University Press, 2008.

Zachar, Peter. "Personality disorder: Philosophical problems." In *Handbook of the Philosophy of Medicine*, edited by Thomas Schramme and Steven Edwards, 1005–1024. Dordrecht: Springer, 2017.

—. "The practical kinds model as a pragmatist theory of classification." *Philosophy, Psychiatry & Psychology* 9, no. 3 (2002): 219–227.

Zachar, Peter, Drozdstoj St Stoyanov, Massimiliano Aragona, and Assen Jablensky. *Alternative Perspectives on Psychiatric Validation: DSM, ICD, RDoC, and Beyond.* Oxford: Oxford University Press, 2014.

# Index

Italicized numbers indicate the pages of illustrations

depression: as paradigm of mental disorder 26, 33, 36, 44, 45f.; construed as a social threat 61; issues in the diagnosis of 98, 107; online therapy for 127; with seasonal pattern 118–119, 122

diagnosis: critique of current diagnostic practices 88–94, 105; ethical complications 36–38, 41–44, 47, 64–67, 74–80, 81, 107; psychiatric diagnosis contrasted with diagnoses of other sorts 86–87; scientific status of diagnostic categories 95–103, 108; variety of diagnostic categories: 4f., 16

Diagnostic and Statistical Manual of Mental Disorders (DSM): criteria for Narcissistic personality disorder 37; criteria for Oppositional defiant disorder 75; general criteria of mental disorder 16, 41, 47; taxonomic aspirations of 79, 95–97, 101, 108, 122; discussion of Histrionic personality disorder in 140

Dissociative disorders 36, 109, 120, 123, 129

distress 37, 38, 91–92

"dormative virtue" 88–89, 105

dyslexia 36, 44

eating disorder 52, 57f., 90, 105f., 120, 123

*Einheitspsychosen* hypothesis 110–113, 114

epigenetics 26, 126

essence: real vs. nominal 100–103

evolution 17, 40, 45–46

existentialism 117, 122

families 56–57

Fanon, Frantz *42*, 47

Female sexual interest/arousal disorder 78, 82

feminism 53, 82, 106, 122f.

flourishing: contested conceptions of 76–79, 82, 88, 119; many faceted nature of 3, 47; social contributors to 41–43, 52–55, 56, 60–61, 63–65, 67–70, 119, 136–138; role of sexuality in 76–79

Foucault, Michel *43*, 48

free will 29, 35

Freud, Sigmund *41*, 43, 47

function, biological conception of 39–40, 45

games 133–138, 142–143

Gender dysphoria 4

Generalized anxiety disorder 4, 47, 86f., 95, 98, 103, 118

Gilbert's syndrome *see* liver disorder

gold *see* natural kinds

goldfish 13–14, *14*

Hacking, Ian 109

hallucination 64–65, 77

heart 7, *9*, 19

hepatology *see* liver disorder

Histrionic personality disorder 68, 127, 140

homosexuality 76, 81

Hume, David 34

hysteria 120, 123, 129, 139

influenza 27

introspection, limits of i, 7, 87, 103

jealousy 87

"knowledge argument" 11–14, 21

laws of nature 29–30, 110–113, 115

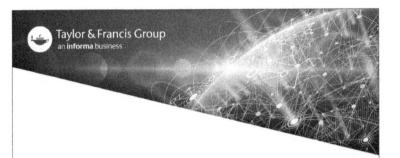